THE BOZEMAN TRAIL

PRUETT P PUBLISHING COMPANY
Boulder, Colorado

The Wagon Box Fight by Bernard Thomas—*Owned by the Sheridan County Fulmer Public Library and reproduced from a photo by John Lyle*

The Bozeman Trail

HIGHWAY OF HISTORY

Robert A. Murray

© 1988 by Pruett Publishing Company

First Edition

1 2 3 4 5 6 7 8 9

Printed in the United States of America

Library of Congress Cataloging-in-Publication Data

Murray, Robert A.
  The Bozeman Trail.

  Bibliography: p.
  Includes index.
  1. Bozeman Trail—History. 2. Bozeman Trail—Description and travel—Guide-books. 3. Historic sites—Bozeman Trail—Guide-books. I. Title.
F731.M98 1988   978.6   88-17848
ISBN 0-87108-734-0 (Paperback)
ISBN 0-87108-758-8 (Hardcover)

Map and Cover Design by Robert F. Wilson

Front Cover Painting: *The Last Look* by Ken Ralston. —*Reproduced through the courtesy of Dr. Edward F. Randak, Billings, Montana*

Back Cover: Cattle roundup *Old Powder River Days.*—*Custer Battlefield National Monument*

To Nettie Wright,
pioneer of organized recreation in the Powder River country.
Nettie brought the first rollerskating rink to Buffalo, along
with many other pleasures for the discriminating citizen.

Contents

Introduction

Travelers new to the west find the distances unbelievable, the scenery new and different, the light blinding, and the kaliedoscopic speed of its historic period development fascinating.

Newcomers have often heard of these trails through stories of individual incidents. But they seldom find sources that capsule the colorful events of the early days along a whole trail system in readable form within a single volume.

It is the aim of this writer to provide such a book about the Bozeman Trail, winding some four hundred fifty miles from jump-off points on the North Platte River to the early settlements of south central Montana. Here, in just ninety years, traders, trappers, explorers, soldiers, Indian warriors of half a dozen tribes, farmers, stockmen, and prospectors passed along its course in an almost constant procession, until railways and graded roads bypassed much of the trail, leaving grassed-over ruts and scattered historic sites to mark its route. We hope that tourists, students and armchair history buffs will find it useful, and the key to many an adventure of their own in the field and in the libraries, over the years.

Robert A. Murray
In Camp Near Goose Creek

Part One

The Setting

The vast sweep of land has changed little since the days of the Bozeman Trail—*Jerry Keenan Photo*

Old Trails On The Plains

The Indians that the fur traders and trappers found here in the early 1800s do not seem to have named the trails they used, taking them for granted as the easiest way through the country. If anyone asked, they might have said as the Crows did about the famed Medicine Wheel of the Big Horn Mountains, "The people who made the stone arrowheads made it," or that the" big game" made it.

But certainly even by the time the Crows began to drive the Snakes out of the region on the east side of the Big Horns during the eighteenth century there was an interbraided network of very ancient trails on the plains. One of the region's master storytellers, Dan Cushman, called the trails that trended southeastward just in front of the mountains from Canada to Mexico "The Great North Trail."

In 1851–1860, an expedition of the Army Corps of Topographic Engineers led by Captain William F. Raynolds put certain trails "on the map"—the first good map of the region. The expedition did not name these trails, but several, including the route from Powder River to Deer Creek; the route from the mouth of Big Horn Canyon to Powder River; and the route from Clark's Fork of the Yellowstone; are parts of what became known just a few years later as "The Bozeman Trail."

Who was this man Bozeman, and how did he suddenly get his name attached to what Raynolds described in 1860 as potentially "a great wagon road," one that would play an important part in settlement of the region some day?

John M. Bozeman was a Georgian. Like many from the old gold–placer regions of that state, he drifted west to the Colorado gold rush, and then on, probably over the Cherokee Trail and the Fort Hall road, to the mining camps of Montana. He described himself in letters to his family as "a speculator." By 1862, he was in the budding a settlements of the Gallatin Valley.

There, like others, he surely learned of the trails explored by Raynolds and Lieutenant Henry Maynadier, as well as others used by trappers and traders, many of whom still resided in the Montana camps.

In the spring of 1863 Bozeman teamed up with another man from the Gallatin, John Jacobs, to reconnoitre the trail network to the southeast. Their aim, to draw off some travelers from the Oregon/California trail on the Platte with the lure of a shortcut to the new settlements of Montana. They wanted to make some quick cash guiding emigrants, and to enhance the flow of people into the Gallatin Valley,

boosting the value of their land holdings and mercantile ventures there.

Bozeman and Jacobs together with the latter's little daughter struck out along the trails that year making their way to the trading posts strung out along the North Platte. The most important of these was John Richard's post and tollbridge near present Evansville, Wyoming, founded in 1853, and well known through the region.

John M. Bozeman.—*Montana Historical Society*

Beginnings Of Emigrant Traffic On The Bozeman Trail

John Bozeman spent some time around Richard's Bridge and Trading Post on the North Platte that spring of 1863. Finally, he assembled a train of wagons that wanted to try the new "shortcut." They set out through the sand-hill country north of the bridge, heading northeast to Brown's Springs, at which point they picked up what was to become the Bozeman Trail's main stem. From here they passed on to the Dry Fork Crossing of the Powder River, then headed northwest, without incident.

On they trudged as far as the Clear Fork of the Powder River. Here the party met a strong force of blustering, threatening Sioux. Had they met this show of force head–on and proceeded with due caution, they probably would have passed through without incident. However, in the party was a notably nervous frontiersman, Rafael Gallegos, always the soul of caution. After listening to Rafael, they panicked and refused to go further without a military escort.

They camped right there and sent old John Bouyer back to Camp Marshall on La Bonte Creek to seek army protection. The army, however, was thinly spread at the little garrisons along telegraph and stage lines, and would not send an escort. So the emigrants turned back to Richard's Bridge, and went on to Montana over the Fort Hall road.

Bozeman, along with other frontiersmen, crossed the Big Horns nearby and made their way to Montana through the Big Horn Basin. Bozeman, himself, would try again next season.

The following year, 1864, would prove to be the peak year of emigrant traffic on the trail.

Marker commemorating the Bozeman Trail.—*Wyoming State Archives, Museums and Historical Department*

Camp Marshall on LaBonte Creek was simply a military expansion of the stage station built in 1859 and expanded with telegraph facilities in 1861, after also serving as a pony express station.—*American Heritage Center, University of Wyoming*

Treaty Status Of Lands
Along The Bozeman Trail

No aspect of Bozeman Trail history has been so distorted as the status of various tribes, with regard to the lands traversed by the Bozeman Trail. The facts are these, as shown by the treaties involved:

The primary treaty document of concern is the 1851 Horse Creek Treaty (often called the Fort Laramie 1851 Treaty). Under its provisions, *the entire length of the trail from all of its starting points lay through Crow territory*, except for the small segment from present Livingston, Montana to Bozeman.

The negotiations involved in the 1868 Fort Laramie Treaty were conducted on this basis. The Crows signed away their rights to the lands south of Montana, retaining only the right to hunt on those lands *so long as game remained in sufficient numbers to justify the chase.*

Beginning in the 1850s the Sioux and Cheyennes began to push their way up the North Platte River. They were lured in part by the trading posts established by their relatives, the Richards and the Bissonnettes, and still more when Major Thomas Twiss, the Indian

agent for the Upper Platte moved his agency from Fort Laramie to Deer Creek to escape military pressures on his relationship with the tribes.

In 1860, the Sioux pushed around the north side of the Black Hills for the first time, and from then on the two prongs of Sioux incursions steadily drove the less numerous Crows back beyond the Big Horn Mountains and the Big Horn River.

It is critical to understand that neither the Sioux nor the Cheyennes have *ever* had any treaty rights in the Bozeman Trail country.

The persistent invasion of Crow territory by the Sioux was as important as any other factor in bringing the U.S. Army into combat with the Sioux in the several wars against them from 1855 to 1877. The Hayfield fight, the Custer fight, and Crook's Battle of the Rosebud were all fought within the limits of the Crow reservation! The Sioux had no business there, and it is small wonder that the Crows sided with the government in those campaigns!

Artist's depiction of the 1868 Laramie Treaty Conference.—*Custer Battlefield National Monument*

Indians of the bison era on march, using dog travois.—*Custer Battlefield National Monument*

Preparing buffalo hides.—*Custer Battlefield National Monument*

A Crow Indian encampment on the Little Big Horn River.—*Custer Battlefield National Monument*

Soldiers on the Bozeman Trail

What kind of men did the army send to the Bozeman Trail country? There are two distinctly different periods involved that we must think of separately.

1865–1868

In 1865–1866, Brigadier General Patrick E. Connor's men were all Civil War volunteers, largely members of units recruited in the various states and territories. Some, members of the Fifth and Sixth U.S. Volunteers, had served in the Confederate Army, been captured and volunteered for the special units assigned to fight Indians in the West. These former Confederates were known as Galvanized Yankees, and were all men with combat experience.

The Nevada, California, and Utah troops under Connor's command also had combat experience fighting Indians along the Overland Stage Route to California through campaigns in Nevada, Utah, Idaho, and southwestern Wyoming. Connor and some of his other officers had served in the war with Mexico nearly twenty years earlier.

The column commanded by Colonel Henry B. Carrington was another matter entirely! Carrington's commission as colonel was a direct political appointment, made when the Eighteenth Infantry was organized in the summer of 1861. The appointment was his reward for helping the Lincoln campaign succeed in Ohio. Carrington had no combat experience whatever, and his command was thus resented by officers who had fought all through the war.

Carrington's officers were a mixed lot, including a few seasoned combat veterans (some from the Mexican War); a lot of mediocrities with varied problems ranging from alcoholism and drug addiction, to mental illness, old wounds and other illnesses. A handful of officers were eager but green youngsters.

Regimental records show that the enlisted personnel compliment contained only a few Civil War combat veterans. Most were young, green kids from the farms of the midwest, the cities of the east and the immigrant depots at the major ports. They received no training at all on the way west, and none during Carrington's tenure at Fort Phil Kearny. While his cavalry contingent was stationed at Fort Laramie on its way up country, the post commander there called it "The worst cavalry I have ever seen!" Such men, led by Captain William J. Fetterman met disaster near Fort Phil Kearny in late 1866.

General William T. Sherman. Sherman commanded the vast military division of the Missouri during the early years of the Bozeman Trail and was later named general of the army when Grant was elected president.—*Custer Battlefield National Monument*

General Philip H. Sheridan. As Sherman's successor, Sheridan was charged with the responsibility of pacifying the western frontier.—*Custer Battlefield National Monument*

After Carrington left Fort Kearny, Brigadier General Henry W. Wessels, with well over twenty years of experience, and Major James Van Voast, an outstanding and experienced officer assumed command at Fort Phil Kearny and Fort Reno respectively. By the spring of 1867, they had made great strides in whipping the green recruits into shape. The new district commanding officer, Colonel Johnathan Eugene Smith and his assistant, Major Benjamin E. Smith (no relation) continued the program and improved upon its record. Other officers such as Lieutenant Colonel Luther P. Bradley and Captain Andrew S. Burt at Fort C.F. Smith, and a generally better class of company grade officers, added to the strength of that force. Consequently, from mid–1867 on, the troops stationed along the Bozeman were very effective, well disciplined, and had good morale.

1876–1894

There was an immense turnover among the privates in the western army during the years 1868–1876. A soldier's state of training depended almost entirely on the attitude of his company commander. Many relatively new recuits were in the units that General George Crook took north on the Bozeman Trail in his 1876 campaigns, but they were intermixed with veterans of Indian campaigning from other regions, such as Texas and Arizona. The contingent Lieutenant Colonel John Gibbon brought east over the Bozeman Trail and down the Yellowstone in 1876 was less experienced, but nevertheless, better on the average than Carrington's men had been. After the close of the major campaigns, the army studied and improved its training methods to such an extent that by 1887 a foreign observer commented that the United States had, man for man, the best trained regular army in the world!

Lieutenant Colonel John Gibbon, commander of the Department of Montana. Despite a distinguished Civil War career, he would be remembered more for his role in Custer's last campaign.—*Custer Battlefield National Monument*

A typical cavalryman.—*Custer Battlefield National Monument*

Scouts by Remington.—*Custer Battlefield National Monument*

The Open Range Cattle Boom

By 1866, stockmen from the midwest and Texas were driving Texas beef herds northward to meet the advancing railroad loading points in Kansas and Nebraska. They soon found that the belt of high plains country all along the foot of the Rockies was prime grazing ground, and that cattle could be wintered in the belt where periodic chinook winds stripped the snow away from the sun-cured grasses of those plains and foothills.

The mining towns of Colorado, as well as the military posts and the Indian agencies of the region provided a sizeable market themselves. Moreover, rails were pushing west to reach the region, and would soon offer ready access to eastern markets.

Consequently, more and more ranchers took up their trade in eastern Colorado and soon pushed into southeastern Wyoming. Texas cattle were very cheap. Beef prices were rising. From 1869 to 1882, a host of "experts" published books and articles showing "How to Get Rich on the Plains," as one author put it.

The game was this: to find a place where the range was not already crowded; pick a sheltered location along some stream, and put up a house and horse shed and bunkhouse. The next step was to hire a foreman and four or five "hands;" buy cheap Texas cattle, and simply turn them loose on the range; anywhere from several thousand to the 25,000 or more some outfits had. The cattle were marked with a registered brand. In spring a group of neighboring stockmen cooperated to round up the stock and identify each calf with the brand of its mother. In fall another roundup was held to select three and four-year-olds for shipment to market. During these roundups, the outfits hired itinerant cowboys, largely Texans. By and large these cowboys were hard working and loyal during their term of employment, but were carefree, footloose lads who had drifted into the work "because you can't do nothin' else!" as one writer put it.

Such ranching outfits had filled up the Colorado Front Range country by 1866 and spilled over into southeastern Wyoming, south of the North Platte River soon after the arrival of the Union Pacific in Cheyenne in 1867. They eagerly awaited the expulsion of the Indians from the country to the north, which was completed by 1877.

Late in 1878, two Englishmen, Moreton and Richard Frewen stepped off the Union Pacific at the desert stop of Bryan in southwest Wyoming. Ostensibly, the pair was on a big game hunting trip, but it quickly became apparent that they were looking for choice grazing ground so they could get into this promising cattle business.

The Upper Green River country proved too high and cold. They looked at the Wind River Basin and the upper end of the Big Horn Basin. Then, in December 1878 they came over the Big Horn Mountains and looked out across the Powder River Basin. This was it!

Richard remained in Buffalo to make local arrangements and get acquainted. Moreton headed for Cheyenne and took the train east to raise the needed money for buying cattle. In the boom atmosphere of the cattle business, eastern investors were just becoming acquainted with the projections of wealth to be had there. It helped that Moreton's wife was Clara Jerome, daughter of a multimillionaire investor, with a "spending allowance" of $30,000 a year (at a time when most American families lived on $600 a year).

Back in Wyoming in the spring of 1879, the brothers selected a headquarters site about fifteen

Englishman Moreton Frewen, who with his brother, Richard, was one of the early ranchers in the Powder River country.—*American Heritage Center, University of Wyoming*

miles up the Powder from the Dry Fork Crossing of the Bozeman Trail. They had half a dozen employees including household help here, and a handful of others in small cabins scattered down the Powder. They bought 15,000 head of Oregon cattle on the Sweetwater, and over the next several years another 14,000 head from various sources. Other big outfits, mostly stockmen from southeastern Wyoming flocked to join them, and the Powder Basin began to fill with range cattle.

When the expanding ranching outfits reached Crazy Woman Crossing, however, they found themselves on a new kind of frontier. From there, on north to the Montana line, small scale farmer/ranchers were making desert land filings along the streams, and fencing their holdings as fast as they could buy barbed wire.

The small outfits had an entirely different operating style. They fenced the lands they owned or had filed on, and irrigated as much land as they could get water to. They raised grain, potatoes, and cut irrigated meadow hay. They also ran cattle on the intervening ridges of dry pasture between the valleys, grazing in common, open range style and conducting roundups, but always having their hay meadows and grain crops as a reserve against hard winters and dry

years. These small outfits ran their business conservatively, and had substantial cash income from the military market at Fort McKinney, and Fort Custer in nearby Montana.

Very quickly, the big outfits got into a speculative boom phase, with thousands of head of cattle bought and sold by people who never saw them. The boom peaked out in 1884-1885, and most big outfits began to experience growing financial difficulties after that. The summer of 1886 was dry, and that fall the post commander at Fort McKinney observed that "The country is full of Texas cattle, and there is not a blade of grass within 15 miles of the post." Then a winter such as the country had not seen in twenty years hit the range country. The small ranchers fared quite well, but the big outfits lost from 20 to 60 percent of their herds. Many went broke and left the country.

Survivors saw opportunity, and began to restock the abandoned range without changing their operating style. They also cast envious eyes at the range used by the small ranchers. The big outfits gained control of the roundup process, and tried to shut out the small ranchers from legal marketing, while at the same time "mavericking" or illegally branding many calves belonging to the small ranchers.

In 1891, the small outfits set up their own

Cattle crossing the Powder River.—*Custer Battlefield National Monument*

organization, and made plans to hold their own roundups the next year, ahead of the Stockgrowers Association roundups. The big operators based in Cheyenne were furious. The most radical of them secretly set up a fund, hired some Texas gunmen, and set out in April 1892 on a raid intented to terrorize the small ranchers of Johnson County. The "Invaders," as they were called, got as far as the Powder River, and killed two small ranchers about twenty miles west of the Bozeman Trail, but word got out, and the settlers accompanied by their sheriff beseiged the Invaders at the TA Ranch, just ten miles off the Bozeman Trail. The big outfits used their political connections to get the troops from Fort McKinney to intervene and escort their force back to Cheyenne. The case dragged on until Johnson County ran out of money with which to continue prosecution, so the Invaders went free. More important, though, the rights of the settlers were now firmly established. The big outfits that remained, adopted new ranching practices and learned to get along with their smaller neighbors. Peace had come at last to the Bozeman Trail country!

Cattle roundup during "Old Powder River Days."—*Custer Battlefield National Monument*

Rock Creek cattle outfit about 1890.—*American Heritage Center, University of Wyoming*

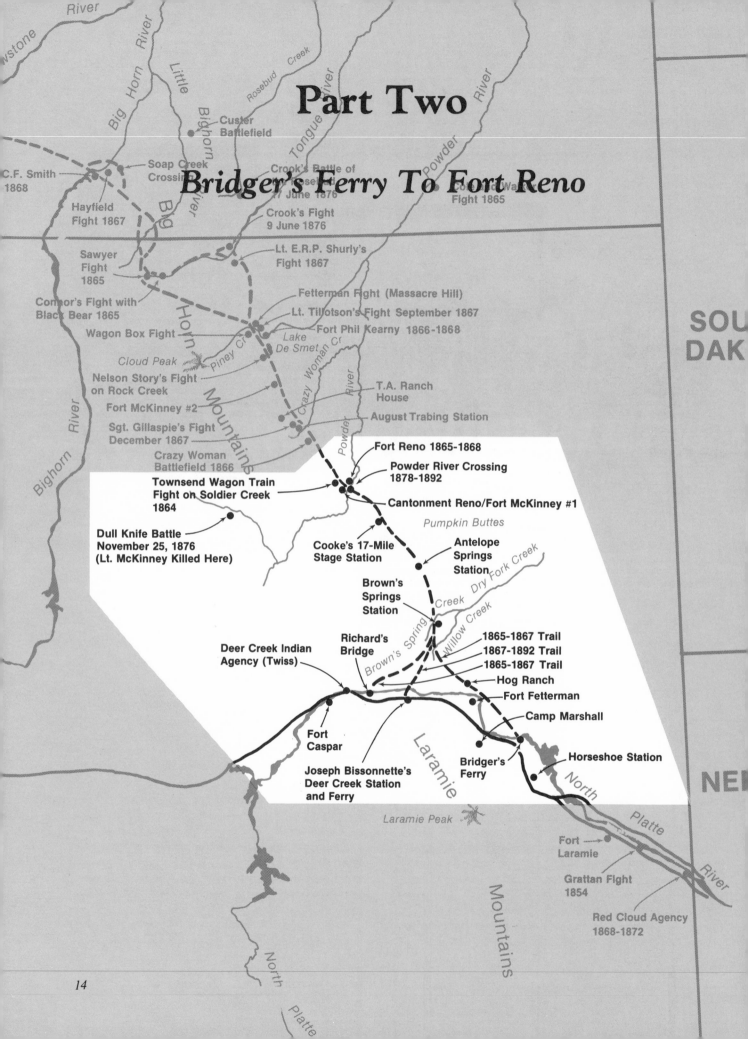

Part Two
Bridger's Ferry To Fort Reno

Yellowstone River

Big Horn River

Little Bighorn River

Rosebud Creek

Tongue River

Powder River

Custer Battlefield

C.F. Smith 1868

Soap Creek Crossing

Crook's Battle of Rosebud 17 June 1876

Powder River Fight 1865

Hayfield Fight 1867

Crook's Fight 9 June 1876

SOU DAK

Sawyer Fight 1865

Lt. E.R.P. Shurly's Fight 1867

Connor's Fight with Black Bear 1865

Fetterman Fight (Massacre Hill)

Wagon Box Fight

Lt. Tillotson's Fight September 1867

Big Horn Mountains

Piney Cr

Lake De Smet

Crazy Woman Cr

Fort Phil Kearny 1866-1868

Cloud Peak

Nelson Story's Fight on Rock Creek

T.A. Ranch House

Fort McKinney #2

Powder River

August Trabing Station

Sgt. Gillaspie's Fight December 1867

Bighorn River

Crazy Woman Battlefield 1866

Townsend Wagon Train Fight on Soldier Creek 1864

Fort Reno 1865-1868

Powder River Crossing 1878-1892

Cantonment Reno/Fort McKinney #1

Dull Knife Battle November 25, 1876 (Lt. McKinney Killed Here)

Cooke's 17-Mile Stage Station

Pumpkin Buttes

Antelope Springs Station

Dry Fork Creek

Brown's Springs Station

Creek

Willow Creek

Richard's Bridge

Brown's Spring

1865-1867 Trail
1867-1892 Trail
1865-1867 Trail

Deer Creek Indian Agency (Twiss)

Hog Ranch

Fort Fetterman

Camp Marshall

Fort Caspar

Laramie

Horseshoe Station

Joseph Bissonnette's Deer Creek Station and Ferry

Bridger's Ferry

North Platte River

Laramie Peak

Mountains

Fort Laramie

Grattan Fight 1854

NE

Red Cloud Agency 1868-1872

North Platte

Bridger's Ferry

From 1866 into late summer 1867, Bridger's Ferry was the most important starting point for Bozeman Trail traffic. Here in 1865, the government furnished the materials and equipment with which Jim Bridger and his associates built a cable ferry across the dangerous North Platte River. At times of particular trouble, the army stationed a company of men at this point and at least one skirmish with Sioux horse raiders took place here.

Bridger left the ferry in the care of others and went up the trail with Carrington in 1866. He was chief guide and interpreter, Mountain District, for which he received $300 per month and expenses (at a time when a private got $13 per month, and an Indian scout $13 a month plus 60¢ per day for his horse).

Bridger's Ferry on the North Platte River. An important jumping-off point for travel north on the Bozeman Trail.—*Wyoming State Archives, Museums and Historical Department*

Montgomery Van Valzah's
Mail Party Massacre

Montgomery Van Valzah was another of the citizens employed irregularly as a mail carrier by the army at Fort Phil Kearny. Late in March 1867, he headed southeast along the trail to Fort Reno and on toward the telegraph line. There were four other civilian travelers along when the unlucky group ran into a Sioux war party on the Dry Fork of the Powder River. In the fight that followed all five whites were killed.

Antelope Springs

One of the reliable watering places on the driest portion of the Bozeman Trail, Antelope Springs, is mentioned in many traveler accounts.

The army had a small outpost here in 1877. It consisted of a dugout house, and a ring of rifle pits on the hilltop just above. Normally manned by a sergeant and three privates, the outpost at Antelope Springs served as an overnight shelter for couriers and telegraph repair crews.

The Rock Creek Stage Line put up a station here in 1879. In March 1887 events at the station put the place "on the map" for the region's residents.

Army Paymaster D.N. Bash and his civilian clerk had taken the stage out of Fort Fetterman the previous day, heading north to pay the troops at Fort McKinney.

The stage made a noon stop at Antelope Springs. Major Bash and his clerk, along with the other stage passengers went into the station for lunch. At this point a cowboy named Charlie Parker grabbed the paymaster's valise from the coach and raced away. The people at the station boiled out like bees from a hive, mounted the stage horses and set out in hot pursuit. Parker outdistanced them easily on his tough mustang.

Months later, under an assumed name, Parker bought a ranch in Nebraska, but his free spending habits aroused the attention of the law, and in a comic opera sequence he was captured, fought a hotly contested battle in the courts, and finally landed in the territorial penitentiary.

The Rock Creek station taken about 1965.
—*American Heritage Center, University of Wyoming*

House Creek

Mike Henry was a true "old soldier." He enlisted as a drummer boy of thirteen years when the Mexican War broke out in 1846, and served thirty years in the regular army, taking his discharge in 1876 at Cantonment Reno.

The frontier was near its end at that time and those who had followed it for a lifetime cast about for new opportunities. Mike knew just the way to build a stake. Here at the mouth of House Creek, on Dry Fork of the Powder River, he did indeed build a "house" called "Henry's Ranche" in the spring of 1877.

It lay just outside the limits of the military reservation, offering most anything a soldier wanted, and who better than a veteran like Mike would know what that was!

A year in business here enabled him to found and stock the 88 Ranch at Brown's Springs and eventually achieve prominence in the open range cattle business.

Mike Henry as a young drummer boy at the time of the Mexican War.—*Wyoming State Archives, Museums and Historical Department*

Ex-soldier and entrepreneur Mike Henry, who built "Henry's Ranche" at the mouth of House Creek on the Dry Fork of the Powder in 1877.—*Wyoming State Archives, Museums and Historical Department*

Grave of John Brown at Brown's Spring.—*American Heritage Center, University of Wyoming*

The Dry Fork Crosssing
Of The Powder River

This bleak sagebrush plain along the Powder River is lonely and windswept today, but a century and more ago, it was a major crossroads for the entire region. Indians trailed through here regularly from several directions. Captain John Weber's mountain men passed up the Powder here on their way to trap in the Big Horns in 1823. Lieutenant Henry Maynadier and his explorers passed here on their way to Deer Creek in 1859. Soon the area became more than just an occasional campsite.

Dry Fork of the Powder River looking southwest. Dry Fork parallels a trail down to the river. Trees have grown over the trails because more moisture is available to them there.—*Margaret B. Hanson*

The German Lutheran Mission Station
On The Powder River

Congregations of German Lutherans who had settled in Iowa, and were well established by the 1850s, decided to send out missionaries to the western Indians. In 1858 a party of these missionaries steamboated to Fort Union on the Upper Missouri where they got to know the Crows.

They decided to locate a mission station in what they believed to be the heart of the Crow country. Coming up the Oregon Trail in the late summer of 1859, they reached Deer Creek, and were welcomed by genial Indian Agent Thomas Twiss.

Close to his agency lay the recently abandoned buildings of a Mormon mail station and supply depot. Twiss told the missionaries they could winter there. The party built a cabin, fenced off a garden space and broke up land to plant. They celebrated Christmas with

Captain William F. Raynolds and headed up the Bozeman Trail in the spring of 1860.

All seemed well under way, but conditions were changing fast on the plains. What had been securely Crow country a few years earlier was now not far from the advancing frontier of the Oglala Sioux.

A party of Sioux visited the station in the summer of 1860, and while they behaved well, the air crackled with tension. Not long after they left, Reverend Moritz Brauinger went out to herd stock, and when he did not return, it was presumed he had been killed by the Sioux. The associates abandoned the station and retreated to the security of Deer Creek, leaving behind the first permanent structure in Wyoming north of the Platte Valley.

The Lutheran mission station on Powder River.—*American Heritage Center, University of Wyoming*

Part Three
Fort Reno To Fort Phil Kearny

Yellowstone River

Yellowstone River

Big Horn River

Little Bighorn River

Rosebud Creek

Tongue River

Powder River

Custer Battlefield

Fort C.F. Smith 1866-1868

Soap Creek Crossing

Hayfield Fight 1867

Crook's Battle of the Rosebud 17 June 1876

Cole and Walker Fight 1865

Big Horn River

Crook's Fight 9 June 1876

Sawyer Fight 1865

Lt. E.R.P. Shurly's Fight 1867

Connor's Fight with Black Bear 1865

Fetterman Fight (Massacre Hill)

Lt. Tillotson's Fight September 1867

Wagon Box Fight

Fort Phil Kearny 1866-1868

Lake De Smet

Cloud Peak

Piney Cr

Crazy Woman Cr

Nelson Story's Fight on Rock Creek

Powder River

T.A. Ranch House

Fort McKinney #2

August Trabing Station

Horn Mountains

Sgt. Gillaspie's Fight December 1867

Fort Reno 1865-1868

Crazy Woman Battlefield 1866

Powder River

Powder River Crossing 1878-1892

Bighorn River

Townsend Wagon Train Fight on Soldier Creek 1864

Cantonment Reno/Fort McKinney #1

Dull Knife Battle November 25, 1876 (Lt. McKinney Killed Here)

Pumpkin Buttes

Cooke's 17-Mile Stage Station

Antelope Springs Station

Dry Fork Creek

Brown's Springs Station

Creek

Willow Creek

Richard's Bridge

Brown's Spring

1865-1867 Trail

1867-1892 Trail

Deer Creek Indian Agency (Twiss)

1865-1867 Trail

Hog Ranch

Fort Fetterman

Fort Caspar

Laramie

Camp Marshall

Horseshoe Station

Bridger's Ferry

Joseph Bissonnette's Deer Creek Station and Ferry

North Platte

Laramie Peak

Fort Laramie

Fort Reno

During 1864, congress passed the Second Pacific Railroad Act, assuring an early construction start for the Union Pacific. Worried, because of Indian attacks on the stage lines the previous season, the secretary of interior insisted on maximum protection for railway surveyors and construction crews. Accordingly, the secretary of war requested opinions from army officers on how this might be best accomplished. One reply stood out as offering the most promise of success. Lieutenant Colonel William O. Collins of the Eleventh Ohio Volunteer Cavalry was just back from two years along the western trails. He said:

> The permanent cure for the hostilities of the Northern Indians is to go into the heart of their buffalo country and hold forts until the trouble is over. A hasty expedition, however successful, is only a temporary lesson, whereas the presence of troops in force in the country where the Indians are compelled to live and subsist would soon oblige them to sue for peace.

Collins went on to recommend that one post should be built on the Little Missouri, near the Missouri Buttes, and another "at some proper point on Powder River."

Hostilities built up fast in the spring of 1865. The army decided to combine Collins' idea with that of another proven Indian-fighter, Brigadier General Patrick E. Connor, who favored a massive punitive expedition into the region.

Connor said that with 20,000 men he could end the Indian question as a military problem on the plains. This did not sound like many men, when at the time he wrote it the Civil War was still on, and there were almost a million men in the Union army!

By the time the expedition was scheduled to assemble, however, the war was over, and political pressure brought about a rapid demobilization. Connor got 2,000 men instead of 20,000. Most of the transportation equipment they needed was in army depots in Missouri, Iowa, and Illinois, a thousand miles away.

It took too long for the expedition to assemble, but at length they got under way, with one column marching up the Bozeman Trail under Connor's direct command. They selected a site about three miles downstream from the mouth of Dry Fork, where there was a good all-weather crossing of the Powder. Their camp lay on the south side of the stream, strung out through the open cottonwood timber for well over a mile.

Patrols ranged out from this camp, and Connor said:

> There is a trail six miles west of here over which they pass, and not being aware of our presence, we sometimes get one. Yesterday my scouts killed one of the principal chiefs of the Cheyennes, and today Captain Marshall, 11th Ohio, killed two Indians.

Soon Connor moved out with most of his column, leaving two companies of Fifth U.S. Volunteers (Galvanized Yankees) to complete construction of a post on the high benchland to the north of the stream from their camp.

Cottonwood trees cut from along the stream banks provided logs needed to build the post. Construction was rough and hastily done, to provide basic shelter before winter. Supply warehouses were erected first, and surrounded with a stockade. When this was completed, they built barracks, offices, officer quarters, and other structures. Save for the supply warehouses, all buildings stood on the open prairie, without benefit of stockade protection.

Brigadier General Patrick Edward Connor. Connor's expedition established Fort Reno in 1865.—*National Archives*

Schonborn's sketch of Fort Reno.—*American Heritage Center, University of Wyoming*

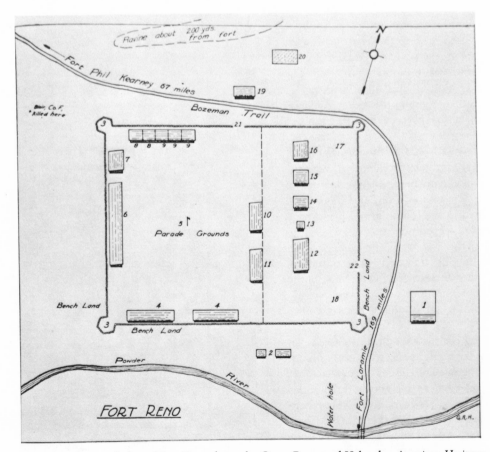

Conjectural ground plan of Fort Reno drawn by Grace Raymond Hebard.—*American Heritage Center, University of Wyoming*

Connor's main force ranged off to the north, and we shall tell of their battle at a later point on the trail. When they came back through the area on the way out of the country, they left Companies C and D of the Fifth USV there, along with Company A, Omaha Scouts (a Nebraska volunteer cavalry unit, actually composed of Winnebago Indians). This small garrison spent an uneventful winter at the post. In June 1866, a column under the command of Colonel Henry B. Carrington arrived to replace them. At first Carrington considered abandoning this post, but then reconsidered, and garrisoned it with a strong three-company force from his Eighteenth U.S. Infantry. At peak of army activity in the region, five companies were headquartered here.

As a number of army sketches and ground plans show, there was almost constant construction and remodeling going on for more than a year, with the post reaching its final stage of completion in October 1867.

Except for cutting hay and firewood, troops at Fort Reno stuck very close to the post when not out escorting supply trains to the posts up country. As a consequence of this, and the fact that Fort Reno had the fortune to have some exceptionally good commanding officers, there was really very little trouble with Indians in the vincity!

The days drifted by slowly along the Powder, with routine formations, fatigue details, construction work, and hours of scanning the horizon, hoping not to see hostile Indians, while looking eagerly for the arrival of supply trains from "The States," and mail carriers who might bring letters from home. Equally welcome were newspapers and magazines to relieve the long hours.

Ruins of Fort Reno.—*Library, U.S. Military Academy, West Point*

From time to time, there would be a brief burst of excitement, as when Chaplain David White and a soldier rode in furiously on July 21, 1866 to tell of their beseiged wagon train on Crazy Woman Creek. Another such instance involved the late night arrival on December 22, 1866 of Portugee Phillips and Daniel Dixon, on their way to the telegraph line with news of the Fetterman Disaster!

As the last of the Bozeman Trail posts to be abandoned in August 1867, Fort Reno quickly fell into disrepair, and much of it burned. In this exposed location it seems likely that the fire was the result of a lightning strike on the prairie. In any case, when General Crook's Big Horn and Yellowstone Expedition arrived in 1876, only two adobe buildings were still standing.

The author on the Fort Reno parade ground. The tree line in the background marks the course of the Powder River.—*Author's Collection*

Sergeant Joe Graham

Already well known for exploits further up the trail, Sergeant Joseph Graham of the Eighteenth Infantry showed the boys how to soldier one spring day in 1867. As fresh meat was always welcome, the post commander at Fort Reno readily acceded to Graham's request to go deer hunting on the bottomlands of the Powder within sight of the post.

As he stalked along, Graham crossed an open tract of prairie. Just then a dozen Sioux boiled out of the timber and swept down upon him. Lesser men might have panicked and lost a scalp, maybe more. But not Joe Graham!

Instead, he calmly sat down on the prairie and began to methodically bang away with his .50–70 Springfield, keeping the Indians at bay until a squad of cavalrymen swept down from the post to drive off the hostiles!

Cantonment Reno (Fort McKinney No. 1) On Powder River

Brigadier General George Crook was a seasoned campaigner long before he came to the northern plains. He fought Indians in California in the 1850s, and in the southwest during the early 1870s. In 1876 he was assigned to command the Department of the Platte, which embraced much of the territory covered by the Bozeman Trail.

Crook's experience with the difficult logistics involved in supporting long range expeditions on the plains had convinced him that this was the main problem in plains warfare. So, in fall 1876, when he took the field with his third and largest expedition of the year, Crook planned well ahead. He sent out three huge ox–drawn trains of supplies from Fort Fetterman over the Bozeman Trail to the Dry Fork Crossing of the Powder River. Each of the trains had an infantry escort, and were under the overall command of Captain Edwin Pollock.

When Pollock's men reached the Dry Fork Crossing, they immediately built timber–framed, canvas–covered warehouses for their boxed supplies, and dug two huge cellars for their potatoes and onions (a quarter of a million pounds of these two essential commodities), and made crude log shelters for themselves. they called their post "Cantonment Reno" after the old regular post of Fort Reno, the ruins of which stood three miles to the northeast down the Powder River.

Crook's men resupplied there both before and after their strike at the Cheyenne village of Dull Knife on the Red Fork of the Powder River in November 1876. Then they moved off northeast to look for more

General George Crook. As commander of the Department of the Platte, Crook spent considerable time on the Bozeman Trail during the ill–fated campaign of 1876.—*American Heritage Center, University of Wyoming*

Indians and filled up their wagons again at a similar camp on the Belle Fourche River. The army had now determined to keep the hostiles out of Wyoming and Montana by almost constant seasonal patrols through the buffalo country. So they kept Cantonment Reno active and made it a "permanent" post, renaming it Fort McKinney, after young Lieutenant John A. McKinney killed in the fight at Red Fork.

Supply trains continued to ply the Bozeman Trail up from Fort Fetterman. Garrisoned mainly by infantry the troops at Fort McKinney managed and guarded the supplies, and set about rebuilding the post for long-term occupancy. Five companies of cavalry also wintered there, building their own quarters. The cavalry spent the summers out on constant patrol of northern Wyoming, charged with the responsibility of chasing stray Indians back onto the reservation.

The site on the Powder offered poor grazing and little ground for a hay crop. Supplies of construction logs and nearby firewood were quickly exhausted. As a result, Pollock cast about for a better site, and early in the summer of 1878, received permission to move the post to a location on the Clear Fork of the Powder River about three miles above its Bozeman Trail Crossing, and just below the Clear Fork Canyon.

The main garrison moved away from the site on Powder River in July 1878, leaving a company to guard supplies and to strip most of the buildings of windows, doors and hardware. The army retained a 640-acre tract here as a campsite, and for some years maintained a telegraph station as well, with a civilian telegrapher and three enlisted repairmen. Ultimately, civilian settlers dismantled the old buildings for construction logs and firewood.

General Crook's supply camp at the mouth of Prairie Dog Creek and the Tongue River, June 1876.—*American Heritage Center, University of Wyoming*

Fort Fetterman: General Crook's departure point for his 1876 campaigns into the Powder River country.—*American Heritage Center, University of Wyoming*

Fort Fetterman, Wyoming Territory: a view from the southwest about 1870.—*Western History Collection, Denver Public Library*

Officers at Fort Fetterman about 1876.—*American Heritage Center, University of Wyoming*

Captain Edwin Pollock commanded Crook's supply trains that travelled the Bozeman Trail during the fall campaign of 1876.—*Wyoming State Archives, Museums and Historical Department*

Colonel Joseph J. Reynolds. Reynolds was in tactical command during the March 17, 1876 attack on the Cheyenne village on the Powder River. Crook later brought charges against Reynolds for the near disaster that resulted from the attack.—*American Heritage Center, University of Wyoming*

27

The Scouting Party by Frederick Remington.—*Library of Congress*

Colonel Ranald MacKenzie's men attacking the Cheyenne village of Dull Knife on the Red Fork of the Powder River, November 1876.—*Custer Battlefield National Monument*

Top left: Captain Guy V. Henry, Third Cavalry, wounded at the Battle of the Rosebud, June 17, 1876. *Top right:* Colonel Ranald Slidell MacKenzie, Fourth Cavalry. The army's premier Indian fighter in the opinion of many. *Lower left:* the celebrated William F. "Buffalo Bill" Cody. *Lower right:* Captain Anson Mills, Third Cavalry also fought with Crook at the Rosebud.—*Custer Battlefield National Monument*

Fort McKinney #1 viewed from the southeast about 1877. *Wyoming State Archives, Museums and Historical Department*

Cheyenne chief, Dull Knife.—*American Heritage Center, University of Wyoming*

The Battle Of Crazy Woman Creek
July 21, 1866

On this day a small column of wagons cleared the horizon southeast of Crazy Woman Crossing and started down the sandy stream bed of a dry wash leading to the crossing. Captain George M. Templeton, commanding, and his assistant, Lieutenant Napoleon H. Daniels rode ahead to check the crossing, and hopefully jump some fresh meat for supper.

When they reached the flat beyond the creek, a party of hostile Sioux suddenly swept down upon them. As they raced for the safety of the approaching train, Daniels fell from his horse, pincushioned with arrows. Templeton took one arrow in his shoulder, but managed to reach the train safely.

Taking command, Templeton led them to the highest point of ground available and circled the wagons. The ensuing fight was unusual on the frontier in reality, but it has served as the classic prototype for Hollywood's endless circled wagon train battles. Troops banged away at the Indians from behind their wagons. The Chaplain led a charge to drive hostiles from a nearby gulch, then, with a companion rode to Fort Reno for help. The officers' wives tended the wounded, while a photographer tried to focus his wet plate camera on the racing savages. Just at the critical moment, a column of cavalry led by Captain David Starr Jordan rode up to the rescue!

Captain George Templeton, Eighteenth Infantry. Wounded at the Battle of Crazy Woman Creek, July 21, 1866, Templeton later served at Fort C.F. Smith.—*Burt Collection, National Park Service, Fort Laramaie National Historic Site*

Sergeant Gillaspie's Fight
Above Crazy Woman Crossing

Veteran Sergeant Amos Gillaspie had charge of a supply train escort of twenty-two men of Company C Eighteenth Infantry. Gillaspie's party fought the last sizeable engagement along the Bozeman Trail in this period, on the first three days of December 1867 when the supply train they were guarding was corralled by sixty Indians a mile north of Crazy Woman Crossing.

Gillaspie's force, and the sixteen civilian teamsters, built breastworks of sacked grain and potatoes from which they defended the train successfully until the arrival of Captain David Starr Jordan's Company D, Second Cavalry relieved the seige.

One soldier was killed in the fight, while three enlisted men and four civilians were wounded.

The Townsend Wagon Train Fight

Only a few trains of emigrant wagons traveled over the Bozeman Trail in 1864. One of these moved under the leadership of an elected captain named Townsend. The train had two seasoned frontiersmen, John Richard, Jr. and Mitch Boyer as guides.

The train, consisting of 150 wagons, together with saddle stock and cattle, left Richard's Bridge late in June and reached the Dry Fork Crossing of Powder River on July 8. On the morning of July 9, they set out again, marching up a small stream called Soldier Creek that came down from the high plains to the northwest. About three miles up the creek they came to a cottonwood grove, and just then sighted a large force of Indians approaching. Boyer and Richard went out to talk to the Indians, learned that they were en route to raid the Crows, and wanted to accompany the train.

The request was refused. Then they asked for food, which Townsend gave them.

However, as one man was missing, Townsend sent a small force out to look for him. The Indians, knowing the man had been killed by one of them, threw down their food, and hand-to-hand fighting ensued. The Indians found the emigrants more than a match and withdrew to the hill east of the grove. They made several attempts to charge the grove, but were beaten back each time by a furious fire from the Henry and Spencer rifles that armed the train. Three emigrant men were killed in the fight and buried at the site. An estimated thirteen Indians were killed. The train continued on to its destination in Montana without further incident.

David B. Weaver and Mrs. W.J. Beall. They traveled over the Bozeman Trail with the Townsend Wagon Train of 1864.—
Wyoming State Archives, Museums and Historical Department

Fort McKinney (No. 2)
On Clear Fork Of The Powder River

Captain Edwin Pollock chose well when he selected the site for the second Fort McKinney in the spring of 1878. Located on a nearly level bench, well above the flood level of deeply entrenched Clear Fork, the site had a well developed topsoil over well–drained rock and gravel layers, the result of an ancient outwash from Clear Fork Canyon just upstream.

Pollock dug an irrigation ditch out of Clear Fork, well upstream, and ran it close around the north side of the post's built-up area. It watered lawns, gardens, and the parade ground, and helped rows of cottonwood trees get a start.

Workmen laid stone foundations, but most of the early buildings were constructed of logs in panels, with timber trusses supporting shingled roofs. Within a few years, the buildings were lathed and plastered inside, and ultimately the logs were covered outside with boards and battens. In due course Pollock erected a water tower, and installed a simple water system to deliver water to hydrants at each set of quarters, barracks, mess halls and the like.

As the construction phase drew to a close, life settled down to a comfortable and orderly pace at the post, with regular patterns of bugle calls signaling roll calls, meals, work parties, drill, and other activities. Formal guard mount ceremonies added color to the day.

Troops seldom took the field in winter. In summer, they patrolled a wide area of northern Wyoming to make sure that no Sioux or Cheyennes were back in the region, and to make certain no hostility developed between settlers and the Crows and Arapaho that still sometimes hunted there.

On three occasions troops from the post had some

Captain W.S. Stanton's surveying party approaching Fort McKinney.—*Wyoming State Archives, Museums and Historical Department*

real excitement. In 1887 on the Crow reservation to the north, a Crow mystic named Wraps-Up-His-Tail (also called Sword Bearer) stirred up a riotous collection of young warriors over the fact that the Indian bureau was interfering with their desultory horse-raiding warfare with the distant Blackfeet!

The Crows shot out windows of the government buildings and otherwise terrorized the agency employees. Troops from Fort McKinney and other posts in the region closed in to make a massive show of force at the agency. The only casualties were Wraps-Up-His-Tail, killed by a Crow policeman, and an old Crow woman who accidentally got in the way of a Hotchkiss Gun shell fired over the heads of the crowd as a demonstration of army firepower!

Things grew more serious late in 1890, when nearly the entire garrison marched off to help supress the famous Ghost Dance uprising at Wounded Knee, South Dakota.

Then in 1892, a strong force of cavalry from the post went out on presidential orders to intervene between the settlers and an invading party of cattlemen and hired guns at the TA Ranch twelve miles to the south. Subsequently, troops from the post escorted the Invaders southeast over the Bozeman Trail to Cheyenne to await trial.

By 1894, the army was well under way with the closing of many small and scattered western posts that had outlived their usefulness. The goal now was to concentrate the troops in larger units at larger posts. So in November 1894, the last of the troops marched away, ending nearly thirty years of military activity along the Bozeman Trail.

"The Line," Fort McKinney, 1891.—*Wyoming State Archives, Museums and Historical Department*

Fort McKinney.—*Joe E. Stinson Photo, American Heritage Center, University of Wyoming*

Buffalo, Pioneer Town
Of Northern Wyoming

When word circulated that the army was surveying the site for a truly permanent post on Clear Fork of the Powder River in 1878, contractors and workmen flocked in to get a piece of the work. Some cut logs in the mountains, others began to stockpile hay; to cut firewood, and to make charcoal for blacksmithing. A swarm of carpenters and laborers began to put up the buildings. Together with the troops, they offered quite a market for many things not stocked by the post trader!

By fall 1878, the post commander reported, "The nearest community is three miles away, a collection of five or six ranches, and is known as Buffalo."

Freighter August Trabing joined with merchant J.H. Conrad and others to found the firm of J.H. Conrad and Company, and open a sizeable mercantile establishment that sold everything from booze to barbed wire. Once at a minstrel show, one actor said "Where would the Devil get a new tail?" The reply was "Why, at J.H. Conrad's of course, they *retail* everything!"

The next spring, several settlers on Rock Creek and Clear Fork made Desert Land Act filings, and began to irrigate small tracts. Many men who had

seasonal construction work at the fort began to take up land in the same manner, and small ranches each built around the nucleus of gardens and irrigated fields, grew up on all the streams from Clear Fork to the Montana line. Buffalo quickly bypassed Big Horn City as a business community.

The army at Fort McKinney bought as much as two million pounds of oats a year to feed its cavalry horses and wagon mules. Two breweries in the town consumed the region's entire 25,000–bushel–a–year barley crop.

All told, by 1887, the settlers had over ten thousand acres of irrigated land in production for grain and produce, much more for hay, as fast as irrigation works could be constructed.

By 1887, the town had over fifty business establishments, plus numerous doctors, lawyers, and three churches. It also boasted electric lighting by 1886, and a city water system by 1888.

From 1879 to the early 1890s, it was the largest town in Wyoming north of the Union Pacific. So long as the army garrisoned Fort McKinney, Buffalo's prosperity was assured!

Returning from the Wounded Knee Campaign, winter 1891, troops march up Main Street in Buffalo, en route to Fort McKinney.—*Wyoming State Archives, Museums and Historical Department*

Buffalo, Wyoming.—*American Heritage Center, University of Wyoming*

The Nelson Story Cattle Drive
At Rock Creek Crossing

Nelson Story was a merchant doing business in the Montana mining country. By 1866, like many other Montanans, he had relocated in the Gallatin Valley. Taking a substantial amount of money in gold, he made his way to Kansas, where Texas cattle were coming up the trails to be shipped east on the railroad. There, he bought a beef herd, filled a wagon trail with merchandise, hired a number of men to manage the train, and a few cowboys to handle the herd. Story then set off for the Gallatin, well over a thousand miles away.

They had many adventures en route, as it took four months to make the trip, with most of the route passing through Indian country. They had one skirmish with hostiles near the Powder River, and two men were wounded. One account says that "A Swede in the party was so badly scared that he died of fright the next day."

Arriving at Fort Phil Kearny, they found Carrington in one of his fearful moods, in which he was reluctant to let them proceed with so few men. Carrington's reluctance notwithstanding, Story early one morning simply pushed on to Montana with his wagon train and herd. After crossing Clear Fork below present Buffalo, they headed up the Rock Creek Valley a short distance to its crossing at a point where the present Interstate 90 crosses the creek. Here a force of Sioux jumped them. The Story party laid down a furious barrage with their Remington–Geiger carbines, driving the Indians up against a steep bluff on the east of the road. Two Indians were killed in the fight, and their bodies abandoned by the fleeing Sioux.

Story left the herd on the good range at the mouth of Shields River, with a few herders in charge, living in a loop–holed log cabin. They had trouble with hostiles and friendlies alike, noting that the Crows could steal horses even when they had the picket rope passed through the loop hole and tied inside the cabin!

About six hundred head of cattle reached the Shields River, but winter losses and Indian raids reduced the number to around two hundred and fifty by the time the beef reached the Montana mining camps.

Nelson Story drove a herd of cattle over the Bozeman Trail to Montana in 1866.—*Museum of the Rockies*

Part Four
Fort Phil Kearny To Fort C.F. Smith

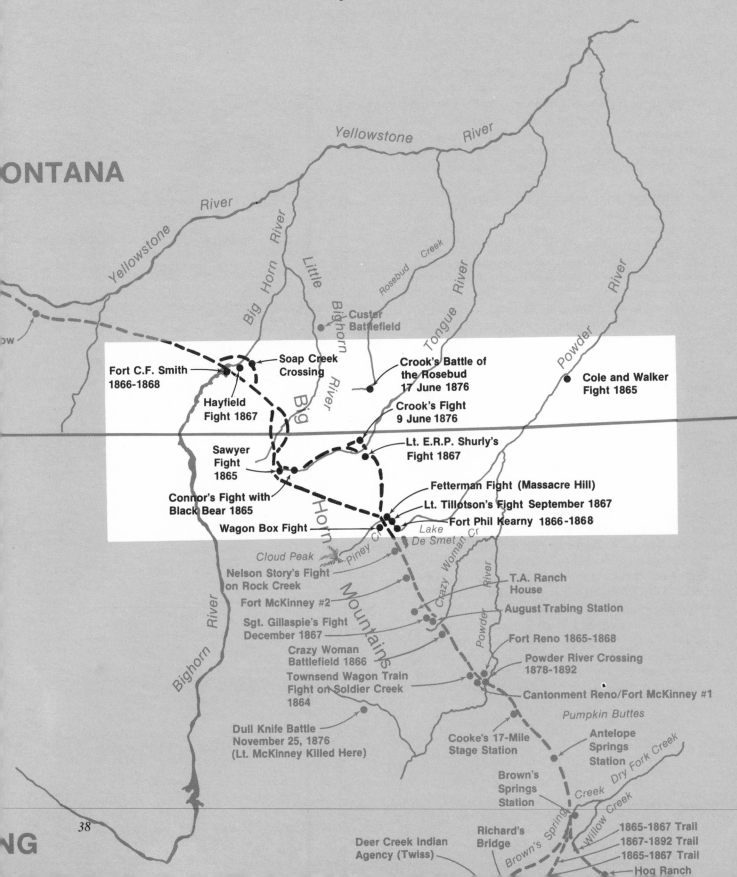

MONTANA

Yellowstone River

Yellowstone River

Big Horn River

Little Bighorn River

Rosebud Creek

Tongue River

Powder River

Custer Battlefield

Soap Creek Crossing

Crook's Battle of the Rosebud 17 June 1876

Cole and Walker Fight 1865

Fort C.F. Smith 1866-1868

Hayfield Fight 1867

Crook's Fight 9 June 1876

Big Horn River

Lt. E.R.P. Shurly's Fight 1867

Sawyer Fight 1865

Fetterman Fight (Massacre Hill)

Connor's Fight with Black Bear 1865

Lt. Tillotson's Fight September 1867

Fort Phil Kearny 1866-1868

Wagon Box Fight

Lake De Smet Cr

Bighorn River

Big Horn Mountains

Cloud Peak

Piney Cr

Crazy Woman Cr

Powder River

Nelson Story's Fight on Rock Creek

Fort McKinney #2

Sgt. Gillaspie's Fight December 1867

Crazy Woman Battlefield 1866

Townsend Wagon Train Fight on Soldier Creek 1864

Dull Knife Battle November 25, 1876 (Lt. McKinney Killed Here)

T.A. Ranch House

August Trabing Station

Fort Reno 1865-1868

Powder River Crossing 1878-1892

Cantonment Reno/Fort McKinney #1

Pumpkin Buttes

Cooke's 17-Mile Stage Station

Antelope Springs Station

Dry Fork Creek

Brown's Springs Station

38

Deer Creek Indian Agency (Twiss)

Richard's Bridge

Brown's Spring

Willow Creek

1865-1867 Trail
1867-1892 Trail
1865-1867 Trail

Hog Ranch

NG

Fort Phil Kearny

Colonel Henry B. Carrington arrived at Piney Creek on July 13, 1866. Together with Jim Bridger and a small escort, he spent two days making a reconnaissance of possible sites over a forty-mile stretch of the Bozeman Trail. Reaching a decision to build on a knoll very near his original campsite, Carrington initiated surveys and started gathering construction materials on July 15.

A number of civilian contractors trailed the column up from Fort Laramie in the hope of obtaining work and more came in with the supply trains as summer wore on. With their work, and that of virtually the entire garrison, Carrington's plans grew to fruition quickly. By early August, he had a 600- by 800-foot area enclosed in a massive stockade of pine logs, and soon after added a cottonwood log quartermaster stockade to this. Building after building followed. Some were very substantial, others hastily built to provide shelter as winter drew near.

Plans for the garrison sounded good, but many problems arose. Food soon became a major concern. Indian raiders made heavy inroads into the beef herds and dairy cows. Coyotes made off with the poultry. Supplies left behind by the Connor expedition at Fort Reno, upon which Carrington counted for winter staples were damaged by insects, rodents, and by poor storage conditions in general.

Carrington found no time for training the men. He did not handle his command responsibilities well, and troop morale sank steadily lower. When Carrington moved on to Fort Caspar early in 1867, following the reorganization of units in the region, Brevet Brigadier General Henry W. Wessels took command. A seasoned combat officer with over twenty years service, Wessels handled the command well, and by the spring of 1867 had done much to rectify Carrington's mistakes.

A new district quartermaster, Captain George B. Dandy, took over the construction work. Dandy made a number of improvements in Carrington's original plan, modified some buildings, replaced some of the temporary construction, and built many new structures.

Margaret Carrington was a brilliant woman, uncommonly well educated for her time, and intensely loyal to her husband. Tragically, she acquired tuberculosis from Henry, who was a carrier, and died of it not long after her graphically descriptive book *Absaraka* was published.—*American Heritage Center, University of Wyoming*

Colonel Henry Beebe Carrington. He would spend the remainder of his life attempting to erase the stigma of the Fetterman disaster.—*American Heritage Center, University of Wyoming*

During the last thirteen months of its existence, beginning in the summer of 1867, Fort Phil Kearny was under the command of Colonel Johnathan Eugene Smith of the Twenty-seventh Infantry. Smith and his staff completed the intensive training that Wessels had begun. They fought the famed Wagon Box Fight and many lesser engagements with skill and determination and always won. They truly brought the Bozeman Trail under the military control Carrrington had only hoped for. More important, they kept thousands of hostile Sioux and Cheyennes tied up in the Bozeman Trail country, and away from the line of construction of the Union Pacific.

After three months of careful planning, and only two weeks after the railroad reached the safety of the Red Desert at the new Fort Fred Steele near Cheyenne, the troops began to move out of Fort Phil Kearny in stages. By mid–August the last garrison troops turned over the fort and its heaps of abandoned supplies to visiting Cheyenne Indians. The Cheyennes lived there a while, and then needing to move and hunt buffalo, set fire to the post lest other Indians take it over!

The legendary guide and mountain man, Jim Bridger went up the Bozeman with Carrington in 1866.—*Wyoming State Archives, Museums and Historical Department*

Fort Phil Kearny as sketched by bugler Antonio Nicoli of the Second Cavalry.—*National Archives*

General Philip Kearny, Fort Kearny's namesake, was killed in the Civil War Battle of Chantilly, Virginia.—*Custer Battlefield National Monument*

General Henry B. Carrington at 1908 reunion at Fort Phil Kearny.—*Wyoming State Archives, Museums and Historical Department*

Sketch of the Fort Phil Kearny cemetery.—*Sheridan County Fulmer Public Library*

In 1888, the remains of the soldiers killed in action at Fort Phil Kearny were removed from the post cemetery and reinterred at Custer Battlefield National Cemetery.—*American Heritage Center, University of Wyoming*

1908 reunion at Fort Phil Kearny. *Left to right*: bugler Pabloski, Lieutenant Wheeler, William Murphy, William Daley, General Carrington, Sam Gibson, Mrs. Carrington, J. Stawn, S.S. Peters, J. Owen.—*Wyoming State Archives, Museums and Historical Department*

Artifacts from the Fort Phil Kearny site, in Gatchell Museum, Buffalo, Wyoming. *Clockwise from lower left:* infantry drumstick fragment; army officer sleeve button; forage cap insignia for infantry cap; hat badge for M1855 dress hat; brassard for cartridge-box sling; infantry .58 minie bullet for M1863 rifled musket; cavalry trumpet mouthpiece; tip for bayonett scabbard; infantryman's shoulder scale; letters and numbers from cap insignia.—*Author's Collection*

"French Pete" And The
First Disaster to Greet Carrington

Pierre Gasseau was one of that sizeable group of traders long associated with the Indians along the North Platte River. Dispensing abundant "Taos Lightning" from small posts along the Oregon Trail, they quickly put the big, older trading posts of the 1840s out of business. Then they began more and more to go out directly to the Indian camps with wagon outfits, feeling secure in their marital connections to the tribes.

Gasseau took one of these small parties north along the Bozeman Trail ahead of Carrington in 1866. When Carrington was just starting construction at Fort Phil Kearny, Gasseau's company was located a few miles to the north where the trail ran down through the country along Prairie Dog Creek and its branches.

Gasseau had a partner, Henry Arrison (until recently the first sheriff of Larimer County, Colorado) and four emplyees from the trader camps on the Platte.

Dispensing liquor and hardware from their wagons, they became embroiled in some sort of argument with their always volatile customers. The young warriors suddenly flared up in anger, and quickly killed the traders.

Carrington went out to retrieve the bodies and buried them as the first in his new post cemetery. Years later they were reburied at Fort McKinney, and subsequently taken to where they now rest at Custer Battlefield National Cemetery.

Tunnel Hill
(On The Horseback Route)

Captain William F. Raynolds, guided by Bridger, struggled up this hill with his wagons in the late summer of 1859. Camping on the Piney beyond, he forecast a "great water power" to be obtained by diverting Piney Creek water over this hill.

Twenty-four years later, settlers did make the diversion, but not for power. Instead they used it for irrigation, bringing 35,000 acres along Prairie Dog Creek into production in just a few years, one element in a homesteader beachhead that the cattle barons could not dislodge.

The Fetterman Fight

Colonel Henry B. Carrington came into the west without a single day's actual field experience in over four years of service. His regiment came with him, short of officers, filled with untrained recruits and with many other personnel problems. He seemed destined for trouble from the start!

The Sioux and Cheyenne were not averse to providing trouble! They began stock raids at Fort Reno just as he arrived there. At Fort Phil Kearny, most of his garrison, civilian employees and contractor work parties scattered out to get construction materials, firewood and hay. They were specially vulnerable to classic small Indian raids.

Carrington and his men responded with hectic and fruitless pursuit of the raiders through the summer and fall of 1866. The Indians grew emboldened by the carelessness and obvious inexperience of the troops.

Into this scene, in late fall, came Captain William J. Fetterman. In contrast to Carrington, Fetterman had been with combat units all through the Civil War. He was brave to the point of foolhardiness, as was his good friend Captain Frederick H. Brown, the district quartermaster.

On December 6, 1866, Carrington led a strong force from the post off into the rough country north of Lodge Trail Ridge, where they soon found themselves engaged in a fight with perhaps three hundred Indians. They withdrew with some difficulty, losing two men. Carrington finally got the message that hectic pursuit could be hazardous to his health!

On the morning of December 19, Carrington replaced the excellent and reliable Starr carbines that his green men of Company C, 2nd Cavalry were just learning to use, and gave them the repeating Spencer cabines of the regimental band. Two days later, these men would ride into combat with the unfamiliar arms!

Carrington needed one more wagon train load of construction lumber to finish the last of his barracks for the season. On the morning of December 21, a civilian contractor party headed toward the mountains to retrieve the logs. When they reached a point on the wood road along Sullivant Hills, about two miles from the fort, pickets scanning the countryside from Pilot Hill signaled that the train was under attack.

Carrington gathered up a small force, and sent Captain Fetterman out to relieve the wood train. For

The Oglala Sioux leader, Red Cloud, architect of the war to drive the army out of the Powder River country.—*Bureau of American Ethnology, The Smithsonian Institute*

Brevet Lieutenant Colonel William J. Fetterman. Fetterman's defeat in the hills along Prairie Dog Creek ranks as the army's second worst disaster in the west, accounting for nearly 8 percent of the army's killed in action in forty-nine years of warfare on the Trans-Mississippi frontier.—*National Archives*

the Indians, this was good news. In their leisurely winter camps where they idled the mild days until winter, they had talked over the events of December 6, and decided to lay an elaborate trap for the careless soldiers.

When Fetterman headed out toward the wood train, the small Indian seige party broke off the action and headed northeast toward Lodge Trail Ridge. Fetterman took the bait and followed. Seeing him veering off toward the hills, Carrington sent out reinforcements. The two groups converged as they approached the ridge. Over they went, with Fetterman and the mounted men in the lead.

Down, along the Bozeman Trail they went, toward Prairie Dog Creek. As they approached the creek, strung out for over a mile, the Indians sprang their trap. About two thousand of them rose up out of the heavy brush along the gullies on either side of the trail, and converged on Fetterman's dispersed force.

In a fierce fire-fight along the branch ridge down which the trail ran, the hostiles quickly overran most of the force driving little bunches of survivors to seek shelter amidst a clump of rocks on the hillside, where they, too, were eventually overrun.

Fetterman, Brown, two civilians and seventy-eight men died there. Milling over the field, the Indians challenged another approaching force under Captain Tenodor Ten Eyck to come down and fight too. Ten Eyck, however, had better sense and returned to the fort with the news.

Carrington panicked, sent John "Portugee" Phillips and Daniel Dixon to Horshoe Station to telegraph the news to the Omaha Headquarters of the Department of the Platte.

The fight marked the worst disaster suffered by the army in the West up to that time. It would take Custer's defeat on the Little Big Horn, ten years later to surpass it. The disaster produced more casualties than all other actions along the Bozeman Trail, combined over a three year period.

Today, a simple memorial marks the site, but the terrain is so rugged that it is easy to reconstruct the course of the action when one stands at the scene.

The Fetterman memorial: reminder of December tragedy.—*Jerry Keenan Photo*

Lieutenant George W. Grummond. Grummond perished with Fetterman on the frozen slopes of Massacre Hill.—*Wyoming State Archives, Museums and Historical Department*

Francis Courtney Grummond Carrington spent about two months at Fort Phil Kearny in the fall of 1866 as the wife of young Lieutenant George Grummond, killed in the Fetterman disaster. After Margaret Carrington's death Francis Carrington wrote a sympathy letter to Colonel Carrington. In due course, their correspondence led to marriage and a long life together. Largely with Henry's aid, she wrote the fanciful and apologetic book, *My Army Life*, published in the 1890s.—*American Heritage Center, University of Wyoming*

Grave of Lieutenant Grummond.—*American Heritage Center, University of Wyoming*

John "Portugee" Phillip's Ride

Carrington's official correspondence written just after the Fetterman Disaster plainly shows signs of extreme stress and near shock that he worked under at this time. Actually his position was quite secure. He had about four hundred and seventy men at the post, including soldiers and frontiersmen taken together. The garrison had more good small arms, and certainly more ammunition than existed in the entire Sioux country. They had four good pieces of artillery and over five thousand rounds of ammunition for them. They were in an excellent defensive position, aware that the only piece of commanding ground lay well within range of the air-bursting shells from their howitzers. Despite the reality of his situation, Carrington penned a panic-filled set of appeals for immediate reinforcement.

The next level of command above the Mountain District was the headquarters, Department of the Platte in Omaha. Carrington wanted to get his messages there as soon as possible. So on the night of December 21, 1866, he hired two civilians at the post to carry his dispatches to the telegraph line at Horseshoe Station, situated on Horseshoe Creek above its confluence with the North Platte River, a few miles southeast of present Glendo, Wyoming.

Folklore has embellished the story of this trip no end, and every year some freelance writer stirs the pot and adds a few items of his own, although the relevant facts and documents have been available for twenty years.

The two civilians hired by Carrington were John "Portugee" Phillips and Daniel Dixon. Neither had been on the civilian payroll of the fort up to this time. Nothing is really known of Dixon, although it is likely that he may have been another of the Montana prospectors. Phillips, on the other hand, was already a well known character in the gold camps of the Pacific Northwest. Born as Manuel Felipe Cartoso, on the Island of Horta in the Portugese Azores, he went to sea at an early age on a Portuguese whaling vessel. They were working in the Pacific in 1849. Putting into San Francisco to resupply, they learned of the California gold rush, whereupon most of the company jumped ship and raced off to the gold fields. It would be years before Phillips would ever see the ocean again!

After a long stretch of learning in the California placers, Phillips (who had early Anglicized his name) and four other Portuguese headed for Linn County, Oregon to seek new placers. From there they went on to the Fraser River rush in British Columbia, then to the Oro Fino in Idaho, and finally to the Boise Basin of

Idaho, where Phillips and another Forty-Niner, Jefferson Standifer, achieved considerable fame as Indian fighters. From here they moved on to the valleys of western Montana. Phillips being a close friend of Standifer joined him in the 1866 expedition to the Absaroka Range and the Big Horn Basin.

At any rate, the pair volunteered to make the trip to Horsehshoe station with Carrington's dispatches for $300 each. They made the trip, returned to the post, collected, and signed a receipt for their pay. Phillips had also negotiated a deal with Colonel Henry W. Wessels at Fort Reno to take messages to Colonel Innis N. Palmer at Fort Laramie. Phillips completed that assignment too.

From Fort Reno to Horseshoe Station, Phillips and Dixon were accompanied by at least three other men, one of whom was James F. Gregory, who later became chief sawyer at the mills that helped build Fort Fred Steele. The trip from Fort Phil Kearny to

John "Portugee" Phillips. With several companions, Phillips carried Carrington's dispatch with news of the Fetterman disaster to the telegraph station at Horseshoe Creek.— *Wyoming State Archives, Museums and Historical Department*

Horseshoe Station was made in three days and ten hours. If the couriers slept six hours each night this is still an average of only 3.69 miles per hour, not a furious ride by any means, but rather one designed to be easy on the horses. Phillips had definitely not ever been down that trail before. We do not know about Dixon. It seems logical, therefore, that the three men who joined them at Fort Reno were familiar with the route to Horseshoe.

We know from military records that the messages went out routinely on Christmas Day from Horseshoe; that they were received in Omaha, and copies sent on to Washington, D.C. We also know that the Omaha headquarters regarded them as ultimate evidence of Carrington's long proven unfitness for such a command. Those are the facts. All else that has been added over the years by way of embellishment is pure prairie frisbee material!

Phillips went on to greater adventure over the years as a gold prospector, logging and beef contractor, and as the proprietor of a road ranch and stage station on the Chugwater. He retired to Cheyenne a wealthy man, dying a peaceful death in his own bed in his big house in 1883. We do not know what happened to Dixon. Phillips years as a road ranch keeper on the "Chug" seem to have been the years in which the "tale grew taller w' the tellin' " as Burns would have put it!

John "Portugee" Phillips marker near Fort Phil Kearny.—*Jerry Keenan Photo*

Sketch by bugler Charles Moellman of Horsehoe Station.—*American Heritage Center, University of Wyoming*

49

Elisha J. Terrill's Grave

Several miles north of the Fetterman Fight site, a lone monument stands within a picket fence on a knoll, immediately adjacent to highway 87, overlooking the junction of two Bozeman Trail branches.

It is the grave of Elisha J. Terrill. A Civil War veteran, Terrill came west to the Montana gold country by another route in the late 1860s. In 1874, Terrill was an important participant in the Yellowstone and Prospecting Expedition that ranged through the country on the Yellowstone, the Rosebud and the western end of the Bozeman Trail, endeavoring to start an Indian war.

In 1879, shortly after the last of the Indian campaigns, Terrill settled down to ranch near this area.

In 1893, Terrill and his neighbors formed the first Fort Phil Kearny Association, dedicated to putting monuments at the fort site and at the Fetterman Battlefield. After fifteen years of persistent politicking, congress appropriated $5,000 for a monument at the Fetterman Battlefield. The monument was dedicated on July 4, 1908, with Carrington giving the main speech and a group of other 1866 veterans in attendance.

Before his death, a few years later, Terrill left a request that he be buried on this spot.

Some ten years ago the place achieved additional notoriety when some wag drove a pair of survey stakes into the cutbank near the foot of the grave and placed a well-worn cowboy boot on each one, stopping traffic on the highway and creating quite a stir. Since that time, the Wyoming Highway Department has placed a steel retaining wall along that bank to protect the grave.

Lieutenant E.R.P. Shurly's Fight

In the spring of 1867, Lieutenant Edmund Richard Pitman Shurly's company went to escort a wagon train about five miles north of Fort Phil Kearny. Shurly's command then accompanied the freighters on up the old branch of the Bozeman Trail, which the freighters preferred because of its easier grades. At a point about twenty miles north of Fort Phil Kearny, they were attacked by a sizeable force of Indians, and had a furious fire fight. Luckily, the troops had a mountain howitzer along, which soon discouraged the attackers. As an officer once observed, "The Indians object to being shot at by a wagon."

Lieutenant Ephriam Tillotson's Fight On The Big Piney—September 1867

Lieutenant Ephriam Tillotson, Twenty-seventh Infantry, with twenty men, took over the guard of a hay camp on the Big Piney about four miles above Fort Phil Kearny on the evening of September 21, 1867. Tillotson's men erected a sod breastwork at their campsite.

Just at the end of the dinner hour the next day, the picket on a nearby hill gave the signal for Indians. About thirty mounted Indians snuck up under cover of brush along the creek, suddenly bursting from cover at a gallop, trying to drive off the mule herd. Troops and part of the dozen civilian haycutters ran into the earthwork and opened fire. All but one Indian from this party swung away and swept through the herd of oxen, shooting arrows at them. The lone Indian kept on with those mules and horses that would run, braving a heavy but ineffective fire.

Meanwhile, another party of twenty Indians swept out from behind a hill and tried to cut off the picket who was coming down from his guard post. He stopped and fired at them, supported by a barrage of fire from troops in the earthwork. At this the Indians broke off the engagement, getting away with sixteen mules and five horses. A board of officers investigated the affair and concluded that the civilian workmen had not hobbled their stock, and that Tillotson had not conducted the defense well, due to inexperience.

The Wagon Box Fight

The Mountain District's new commander, Colonel Johnathan Eugene Smith of the Twenty-seventh Infantry arrived at Fort Phil Kearny early in July 1867. He immediately strengthened Brigadier General Henry W. Wessel's procedures for managing forces both in the field and in garrison.

Smith brought along an ample supply of the new Model 1866 Springfield rifle, caliber .50–70–450. It was a conversion of the Civil War Springfield, with a simple "trap–door" breech mechanism fitted and the barrel sleeved and chambered for the new Martin Bar–Anvil Primed centerfire cartridge. In contrast to the three rounds per minute aimed fire possible with the .58 Springfield rifle musket, the new rifle could fire up to twenty rounds per minute in the hands of a good marksman; it had a much flatter trajectory; and was a much more accurate long range weapon.

Smith and his staff along with most of his officers were seasoned combat veterans with extensive Civil War experience. They soon set up a system of sending a company of infantry up to the area where wood contractors were at work, to take up a defensible position, and provide a secure base from which to protect the workmen.

Late in July, Captain James Powell and his company were on this duty. Powell established camp about a mile from the foot of the Big Horns, on a high, open ridge that commanded a view of the timber operations and controlled their own access to water on Big Piney, about five miles from Fort Phil Kearny.

The Sioux and Cheyennes gathered in large camps each summer for their traditional Sun Dance ceremonies. During this period it was customary to set out on a collective raid against tribal enemies, once the dancing was done.

At the 1867 Sun Dance there was much discussion of the overwhelming success of the Fetterman affair the previous winter. Because of this it was decided to try the decoy/ambush trick again. Accordingly, one large force of warriors set out for Fort C.F. Smith and another for Fort Phil Kearny.

The civilian woodcutters refused to camp with the troops, and set up camp at the foot of the mountain a mile away. Having noted increasing Indian signs in the area, Powell's little command remained on alert. The troops arranged a number of wooden wagon boxes (removed from the running gear so the latter could be used for hauling logs) in a rough oval at the crest of the ridge on which their camp was located. They stacked boxes of hardtack, bacon, sacks of beans, and feed grain to improve their barricade. They had a good

Colonel Johnathan Eugene Smith, Twenty–seventh Infantry, assumed command of the mountain district and Fort Phil Kearny in July 1867.—*American Heritage Center, University of Wyoming*

reserve supply of ammunition for their single shot, breech–loading .50–70 Springfields, although the woodcutters at the camps were armed mostly with government surplus Spencer repeaters.

Around 9:00 A.M. on August 2, 1867 a swarm of mounted Indians swept across the open ground lying south of the infantry camp, driving off a few head of stock grazing there. The men gathered quickly in their defensive position. Powell found he had a combined force of thirty–two soldiers and civilians.

Very soon a large number of Indians, some of foot, others on horseback, charged his position from the east and southeast. The men in the little field fortification stood fast, laying down a careful and disciplined fire with their Springfields and Spencers.

The Indians charged twice more on foot, getting close enough to sink arrows into the wagon boxes. But the fire from the corral was inflicting more casualties than they cared to tolerate, so the attackers withdrew and laid seige to the place, maintaining a constant long range fire, to which the defenders replied carefully and deliberately.

As the fighting wore on, a picket in the lookout post atop Pilot Hill spotted the huge cloud of blackpowder smoke rising from the fight, and signaled trouble to the fort. Colonel Smith immediately sent Major Benjamin F. Smith with 110 men and a mountain howitzer to Powell's relief.

Smith marched up the wood road along the crest of Sullivant Hills, to a point about half a mile east of the present television repeater station at the west end of that ridge. From here, the relief column saw a huge crowd of Indian women, children, and teenagers observing the fight. Smith formed a skirmish line, wheeled the howitzer around, and air–burst a shell in front of the charging Indians. At this, the whole mob broke and ran off to the north across the valley of the Piney and into the hills beyond, followed by the beseiging warriors.

Powell's thirty–two–man force suffered three men killed and two wounded. Powell estimated that at least 800 Indians were actively engaged in the fight, and that his men might have killed as many as sixty of them, but it was enough. Most important, from this point on, the Indians grew cautious in their contact with the troops, and the men's morale recovered from the depths of the despair to which they had sunk after the Fetterman affair. The army was truly in control of the Bozeman Trail once again.

Captain James Powell, Twenty–seventh Infantry directed the defense at the Wagon Box Fight on August 1, 1867.— *American Heritage Center, University of Wyoming*

Looking toward Fort Phil Kearny from the site of the Wagon Box Fight.—*Jerry Keenan Photo*

The late historian, Maurice Frink at the Wagon Box Fight marker.—*Jerry Keenan Collection*

Sergeant Sam Gibson, a participant in the Wagon Box Fight taken at Camp Proctor on the Yellowstone River about 1891.—*American Heritage Center, University of Wyoming*

Sketch of the wagon box corral drawn from data supplied by Sam Gibson.—*National Archives*

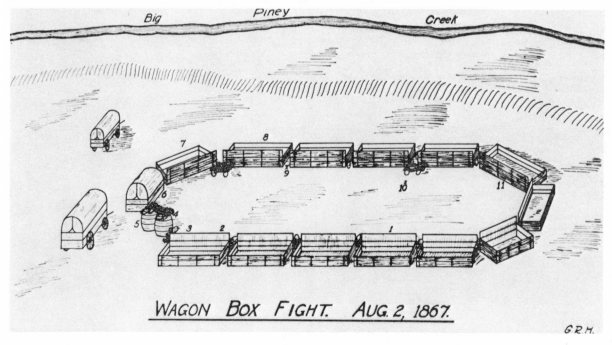

Corporal Max Littman, another participant in the Wagon Box Fight.—*American Heritage Center, University of Wyoming*

Artist Theodore Pitman's conception of the Wagon Box Fight. —*American Heritage Center, University of Wyoming*

Skirmishes Along The Bozeman— Late 1867

Army success in the Wagon Box and Hayfield fights early in August 1867 restored troop morale, and taught the men that if they would only stand fast, aim carefully, and maintain good fire discipline, they could withstand almost any force the Indians might muster. The men gave a good account of themselves from then on out through the rest of the period of the Bozeman Trail diversionary operation.

Usually their wagon trains moved wherever they needed to move without hindrance, guarded by escorts that seldom exceeded thirty men. Often they took along a mountain howitzer.

Captain Henry B. Freeman with an understrength company and a howitzer easily beat off a large Sioux force near Connor's Springs on August 13, 1867.

Lieutenant F.F. Whitehead with a still smaller force routed Indian attackers while in the field near Fort Reno the next day.

Captain Andrew S. Burt with a small force of recruits, and the teamsters of his wagon train, beat off a force of over fifty Indians in an hour–long fire fight in the moonlight at Crazy Woman Crossing about 2:00 A.M. on November 13, 1867.

Casualties from this point on were almost entirely limited to stray individuals who had wandered too far from their outfit, and careless individuals traveling the trail alone or in pairs.

Big Horn City

Here at the crossing of Little Goose Creek, the Rock Creek Stage Line established a station and blacksmith shop in the spring of 1879, and it quickly attracted other businesses. Skinner and Sackett set up business as retail merchants. By 1881, they had put up their new Big Horn Mercantile building, which is still in business today after more than a century of service as a typical frontier store and postoffice.

Bypassed by the railroad, Big Horn City saw its newspaper, the *Big Horn Sentinel*, its college, the Big Horn Collegiate Institute, and other ambitious projects slip away, but the place hangs on, sometimes quiet and sometimes wild, as old time towns can be!

The Upper Crossing Of Big Goose Creek

Here, in mid–September 1866, occurred a small skirmish that changed many facets of history in this region.

Montana placer prospectors were ranging far and wide along the eastern plains in search of new gold deposits. In summer 1866 a party of over one hundred and fifty men left Bozeman and headed east, prospecting the creeks that drained the Absaroka Range. Up through the Big Horn Basin the party moved, working each creek they passed. Reaching the Owl Creek country, they ran into a similar party from Idaho. The groups joined up, then split, and finally came together again, but in smaller units.

One of these small groups elected Robert Bailey as its captain, prospected the streams all along the western base of the Big Horns, then worked the high country. In his 1866 report at the end of that summer, Colonel William B. Hazen noted that "From Crazy Woman onwards, all of the streams are discoloured by the workings of prospectors."

The Bailey party came down from the mountains near here in September 1866, and began to work the creeks along the northeast base of the Big Horns. One morning two men remained behind, planning to go hunting and provide the camp with fresh meat. When the others returned from prospecting they found that both men had been killed by Indians, and buried them on a nearby hill.

The party then continued its exploration, moving southeastward along the mountains. Suddenly, on Prairie Dog Creek they found to their surprise, crews of men cutting hay with mowing machines, and learned about Fort Phil Kearny. Hastening on to the new post, the prospectors found they could make far more working for the contractors and for the army, than their meager prospecting yielded that summer.

Some, like Robert Bailey signed on with the quartermaster at the post. Bailey became post guide at a substantial salary. Others, such as veteran prospector John "Portugee" Phillips, rode shotgun to guard the haycutters from Indian attack. Many of these men figured prominently in the events along the trail over the next two years. Some remained in Wyoming and Montana as permanent settlers.

Connor's Fight On Tongue River

General Patrick Connor's thousand-man column ranged north along the Bozeman Trail late in the summer of 1865, a screen of Pawnee and Winnebago scouts out in advance, searching for Indian sign. They came down the ridges between Prairie Dog and Little Goose creeks, crossed Tongue River, following it upstream toward the mountains. The scouts spotted a large Arapaho camp in a sweeping bend of the river and early on August 29, launched a surprise attack that caught the Arapahos completely off guard. The cavalry swept through the camp, inflicted heavy casualties, and drove off the Arapahos. While this was going on, the scouts scooped up the Arapaho horse herd that grazed on the nearby prairie. Later, the troops collected all of the Indian supplies and burned it, tons of it! A few days later, the now destitute Arapahos made contact with the column. Connor was in a powerful negotiating position, and finally returned most of the Arapaho horse herd after extracting solemn promises of good behavior from the tribe.

This was Connor's last contact with the hostiles. He ranged about seventy miles into Montana, but could not find more of them. Then, word reached him that he was being recalled from the field, because quartermaster corps accountants had found that transportation cost alone on his supplies was running over a million dollars a month, and he had already overspent the quartermaster budget for the entire fiscal year! Connor left his bulk supplies and most of the ammunition at Fort Reno, and his artillery at Fort Laramie, where they would be picked up by Colonel Henry B. Carrington's column the following summer.

Little Horn Crossing

Here in February 1867 began the most dramatic part of the most heroic episode on the Bozeman Trail!

After the Fetterman disaster, Colonel Carrington, strangely enough, made no attempt to send the news to the garrison at Fort C.F. Smith. The news reached the Montana settlements by various means, but the troops at C.F. Smith sat in their winter isolation, worried and disturbed by rumors brought in by the Crows.

Brigadier General Henry W. Wessels, new district commander, tried repeatedly to send mail parties to the Montana outpost, but deep snow and hostile Indians turned them all back. Civilian employees refused to go for less than $1000 each.

Finally, Wessels found that two veteran infantry sergeants, George Grant and Joseph Graham, who agreed to make the trip for $300 each! They set out on snowshoes, sticking to the screening timber of the foothills until they were past what they believed to be the range of the hostiles from their camps on the Tongue and the Little Horn. The pair reached Fort C.F. Smith without incident.

The post commander furnished them horses for the return trip, and also added civilian guide and interpreter Mitch Boyer to the party, placing him in charge. Accompanied by a mule with a packsaddle full of outgoing mail the trio set out on its return trip. On the Little Horn, they were jumped by a small Sioux war party. They raced for the rough country and timber of the Big Horns pursued by the Sioux who stalked them through the woods. They killed some Sioux in scattered little fire fights, but got separated themselves and trudged into Fort Phil Kearny a few days later, heroes if ever there were heroes. Neither of the sergeants ever got paid for the trip. After five years of complaining, Grant was finally awarded the Congressional Medal of Honor for his part in the venture.

Brigadier General Henry W. Wessells replaced Carrington as commander of Fort Phil Kearny.—*National Archives*

Minton "Mitch" Boyer. A highly regarded scout, Boyer was a half-blood Sioux who died with Custer at the Little Big Horn.—*National Archives*

Part Five

Fort C.F. Smith to Virginia City

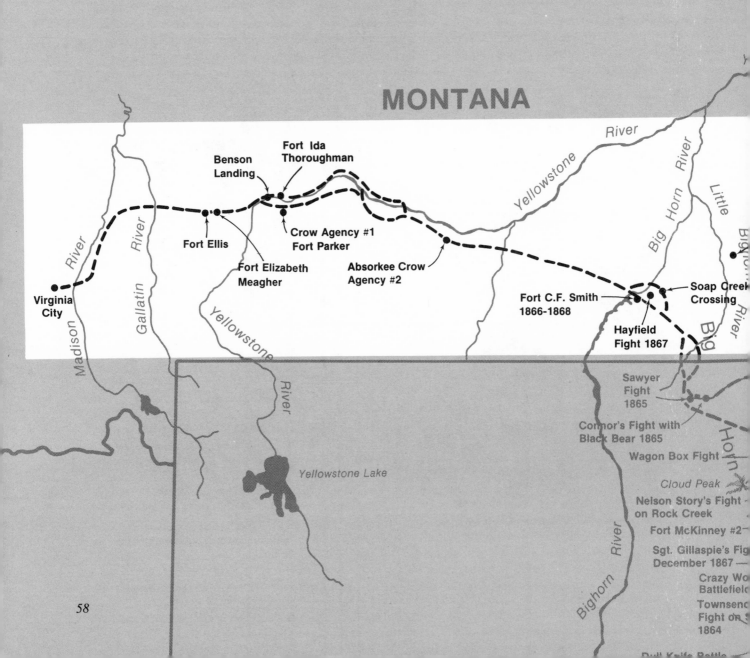

MONTANA

Yellowstone River

Big Horn River

Little Bighorn River

Benson Landing

Fort Ida Thoroughman

Fort Ellis

Crow Agency #1
Fort Parker

Fort Elizabeth
Meagher

Absorkee Crow
Agency #2

Virginia
City

Madison River

Gallatin River

Yellowstone River

Fort C.F. Smith
1866-1868

Soap Creek
Crossing

Hayfield
Fight 1867

Sawyer
Fight
1865

Connor's Fight with
Black Bear 1865

Wagon Box Fight

Cloud Peak

Nelson Story's Fight
on Rock Creek

Fort McKinney #2

Sgt. Gillaspie's Fig
December 1867

Crazy Wo
Battlefield

Townsend
Fight or
1864

Yellowstone Lake

Bighorn River

Fort C.F. Smith

Fort C.F. Smith had a very different orientation from its companion posts downtrail toward the States. In many ways it was a sort of central pivot point on the trail. The most important traffic arriving at Fort Smith from the west consisted of Montana frontiersmen reaching out to the east, prospecting, exploring, hunting, and hoping that the presence of the army at Fort C.F. Smith, along with the powerful force of friendly Crows in the area would provide a protective screen behind which they could lay the groundwork for occupation and development of the upper Yellowstone Valley as a bridgehead for the opening of the whole region to settlement. They also generated considerable traffic by furnishing many of the bulk supplies required by the garrison. So functionally for them, Fort C.F. Smith was an eastern outpost beyond their frontier of settlement.

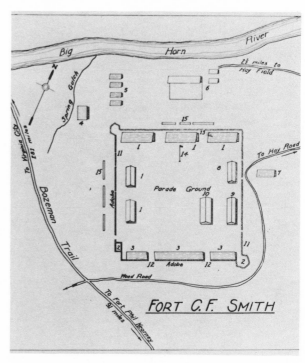

Fort C.F. Smith, late in 1867, as sketched by Anton Schonborn, an army–civilian topographer/delineator.—*National Archives*

Conjectural ground plan of Fort C.F. Smith drawn by Grace Raymond Hebard.—*American Heritage Center, University of Wyoming*

Ruins of Fort C.F. Smith about 1920.—*American Heritage Center, University of Wyoming*

Lieutenant Colonel Andrew S. Burt about 1888. As a young officer, he saw service at Fort C.F. SMith, and later fought with Crook at the Rosebud.—*National Park Service: Burt Collection, Fort Laramie National Historic Site*

Elizabeth Reynolds Burt about 1862. As a young bride, Elizabeth travelled the Bozeman Trail with her soldier husband. Her diary later served as the basis for an excellent account of military life on the western frontier.—*National Park Service: Burt Collection, Fort Laramie National Historic Site*

Elizabeth Reynolds Burt about 1902.—*National Park Service: Burt Collection, Fort Laramie National Historic Site*

Edith Burt, daughter of Andrew and Elizabeth Burt.— *National Park Serivce: Burt Collection, Fort Laramie National Historic Site*

The Crow Indians And Fort C.F. Smith

From 1866 to 1868, many Crows camped near Fort C.F. Smith, and enjoyed a good relationship with the army. Crow hunters supplied buffalo meat to the army, and sold souvenir items, both to the garrison and passing army columns as well. The army in turn furnished the Crows with staple items from its quartermaster stocks. Crow warriors such as Iron Bull served often as mail couriers from the post to and from forts Phil Kearny and Ellis. Far ranging Crow scouts also kept the army apprised of hostile Sioux movements.

Chief Iron Bull of the Crows.—*Burt Collection, Fort Laramie National Historic Site*

Crow Indian encampment.—*Custer Battlefield National Monument*

The Hayfield Fight

The Hayfield Fight, together with the Wagon Box Fight discussed earlier was part of one of the few concerted efforts ever mounted by any significant number of Indians of the region against the army. Most Indian war actions unfolded in an unplanned way as a result of surprise contacts with patroling troops. The summer of 1867, however, proved an exception, when one large force of Indians headed for Fort Phil Kearny, and another, consisting of roughly eight hundred warriors, went to Fort C.F. Smith. In each instance, strategy was to attack a small working party, and if possible destroy it, while luring another force from the fort for a big fight in a replay of the Fetterman affair that had made such an impression on the Indian mind.

The hostiles force reached Fort Smith on August 1, 1867 and discovered a small force of civilian hay-cutters cutting hay on the Big Horn River bottom, some three miles below the post. A few soldiers were on hand to guard the workmen's camp.

Located on open ground, easily vulnerable to a mounted attack, the camp had nonetheless been rendered highly defensible. The men had surrounded their quadrangle with a barricade of logs and posts, interwoven with brush and tree trimmings.

As usual, the Indians gave away their presence prematurely. Citizens and soldiers retreated into the corral, and took up their positions behind the logs of the barricade's lower tier. The Indians charged down on the positions several times, only to be met by a disciplined and determined fire from the same kind of .50–70 Springfields that would be used the following day at the Wagon Box Fight.

Over a period of several hours, the defenders lost three men killed and as many wounded, while killing about sixty of the Indians. By this point the noise of firing, and particularly the rising cloud of smoke from the blackpowder weapons was noticed at Fort Smith. Lieutenant Colonel Luther P. Bradley, commanding the post, sent out a rescue force of about a hundred men and a mountain howitzer. As at the Wagon Box Fight, a single air–burst spherical case shot was sufficient incentive for the Indians to break off the engagement and flee the area. Once again, discipline and marksmanship were found to be the master of the Indian enemy!

General Luther P. Bradley. As a lieutenant colonel, he commanded Fort C.F. Smith.—*National Park Service: Burt Collection, Fort Laramie National Historic Site*

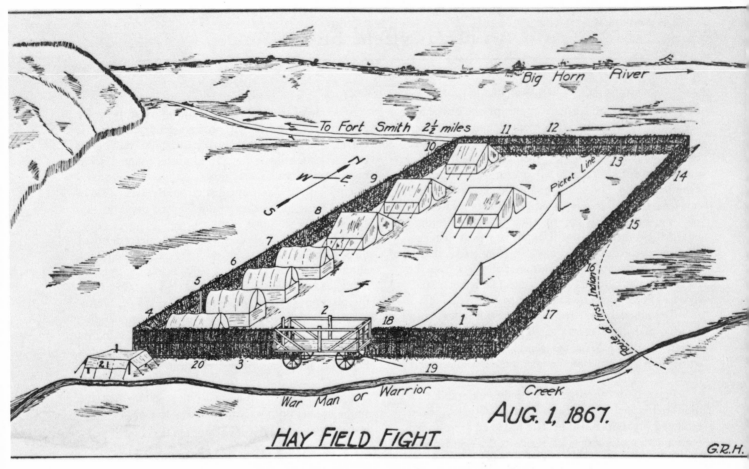

Sketch of the Hayfield Fight, August 1, 1867, drawn by Grace Raymond Hebard from data furnished by F.G. Burnett. Figures indicate positions of fighters. (1) Captain Colvin; (2) Lieutenant Sternberg killed; (3) Al Stephens; (4) F.G. Burnett; (5) George Duncan; (6) Man located here who lost his nerve and never fired a shot during the battle; (7) Bob Little; (8) Holister wounded; died next day; (9, 10, 11) Soldiers; (12) Soldier killed; (13) Soldier stationed her who lost his nerve and threatened to commit suicide; (14) Soldier wounded with arrow; (15) Zeke Colvin; (16) A sergeant wounded in shoulder, fought bravely throughout battle; (17) Billy Hanes; (18) Soldier; (19) Sioux chief killed here by Captain Colvin; (20) Soldier known as "Scotty," wounded; fought desperately through engagement; (21) Cook tent at lower left, outside corral.—*American Heritage Center, University of Wyoming*

Skirmishes On The Yellowstone And Bozeman Trail To Fort C.F. Smith—1864-1877

The most widely circulated works on the Bozeman Trail have focused closely on events on the three military posts (forts Reno, Phil Kearny, and C.F. Smith), and on the segments of the trail between them. This is not entirely a surprise, though it does ignore the intense level of activity on the trail between Fort C.F. Smith and Bozeman.

A critical point seems to be that for Montanans, the Bozeman Trail was not nearly so much a route over which many people would reach their region, but rather a route over which they could explore, prospect, and as soon as possible push their frontier of settlement over Bozeman Pass and down the Yellowstone, as an extension of the *eastward moving Montana frontier* that characterized their pattern of settlement from the coming of the first stockmen and prospectors in the 1850s.

The frequency and persistence of their activity in the region along the trail brought them into contact with the hostile Sioux, who were just beginning to extend their raids into the area in the mid-1860s. This warfare was of such an intensity that it gave the area a much more turbulent history than that of the Bozeman Trail southeast of Fort C.F. Smith.

Many writers act as though the years 1868-1876 were years of peace on the northern plains, when in fact nothing could have been further from the truth, particularly on the Montana frontier! The records of the Crow agencies show a continuous pattern of depredations by the Sioux on the Montana frontier in those years, and the commissioner of Indian affairs was among the loudest of voices favoring a military solution to "the Indian question." In fact, between the Big Horn Crossing near Fort C.F. Smith and Bozeman during the period 1864-1876, fifty-one white persons were killed by hostile Indians and ten were wounded. There is not an accurate count of Crow casualties in the same period, but they were probably higher!

Village of Sioux chief Spotted Eagle on the Tongue River, 1879.—*L.A. Huffman Photo, Custer Battlefield National Monument*

Beauvais Coulee—
Bad Luck On The Prairie!

Beauvais Coulee is a deep, steep-walled drywash that runs down off the northern shoulder of East Pryor Mountain, and angles off northeastward through the high benchland that lies between the Big Horn River and Pryor Creek. A landmark to 180 years of prairie travelers, Beauvais Coulee was first visited by John Colter in 1807. The coulee had acquired a reputation as a place of danger by the 1870s, when the Sioux raiders were pushing deep into the Crow country.

At this same time, the Crow agency on Mission Creek (Fort Parker), and Benson's Landing on the Yellow stone became principal outfitting points for the wolfers: hardened frontiersmen who made their winter living by trapping, poisoning, and shooting the great gray wolves that followed the buffalo herds. Two of these men, Joseph Lee and George Ackerly worked out of the Crow agency. In fall 1873, they headed east to work the country near the Big Horn. They did not return.

In April 1875 Harris B. Hubble, Charley Cocke, and a man known only as Woody headed east with eight horses, traps, provisions, and abundant ammunition for their .50-70 Springfields. They followed the Bozeman Trail to the point where it crossed Beauvais Coulee, just above the big bend the coulee makes to the northeast. In the bend they found some bare standing lodge poles and scattered camp gear along with tattered bits of wolf skins and some human bones.

They concluded that this was the last camp of Lee and Ackerly. From bullet holes in some of the lodgepoles, they deduced that the Sioux snuck up on the camp from the northwest, and from the rim of the coulee, fired into the tipi when Lee and Ackerly were inside, killing them and then looting their camp. It would have been very much in character for the Sioux!

The three trappers went into camp about three miles down the coulee in a small clearing surrounded by chokecherry bushes. At this season runoff water was coming down the channel of the wash and beaver were damming up the seasonal flow. The men scattered out to set traps at these small impoundments.

The next day Cocke was skinning a beaver, and just chanced to look up and see many mounted Indians bearing down on him. Several of them fired at him, and he returned fire, killing one of their horses then ducked into the brush and worked his way back to camp. About the same time he heard heavy firing from up the creek, and knew that Hubble was also fighting his way back to camp. And what a fight it was, with two hundred Indians in pursuit! Hubble hit four of them, with two being probable kills. The Indians grew cautious. Cocke and Woody now in camp had piled up their saddles and supplies into barricades by the time Hubble reached camp. The fight continued, with repeated attempts by the Sioux to overrun the position. The trappers stood fast, however. Firing slowly and deliberately, they killed several of the Indians and wounded many more.

Finally, having suffered more casualties than they would tolerate, the Indians withdrew. The trappers hiked to the Crow agency, where a few days later a party of Crows came in to report signs of many Sioux, with thirteen dead ones in the trees and brush of the coulee! The trappers, like most men of the Upper Yellowstone in those years, were formidable opponents!

The Death Of John Bozeman

John Bozeman described himself in letters to his family as "a speculator" and indeed one had to be to survive on the Montana frontier after the great early 1860s placers played out! By 1867 he was well settled in the Gallatin Valley. In March of that year, he and a business associate, Tom Coover set out for Fort C.F. Smith to solicit contracts for grain, potatoes, onions, and beef at the post.

They spent their first night at Louis Richard's cabin at Benson's Landing, on the Yellowstone. During the night, prowling Indians stole a horse very near the cabin. Richard said that there were Sioux war parties in the region, and advised them to travel at night, advice they disregarded.

At noon the next day, they stopped to cook lunch at a point not far east of Mission Creek. Six Indians approached them on foot. Coover started to get their horses. Bozeman stopped him, saying "They are Crows," but when the Indians came within two hundred yards, Bozeman said "I don't think they are Crows. You get the horses, and I'll stand them off!" Coover went for the horses. However, the Indians still had their guns encased, and Bozeman may have thought there was a chance they might yet be Crows, for he let them approach to within fifteen feet. Just then one Indian raised his gun, fired the weapon through its cover and killed Bozeman.

Coover charged down on then, firing his revolver. The Indians retreated, and Coover grabbed his own rifle from near Bozeman. Seeing Bozeman dead, he retreated to the brush and carefully made his way to Richard's cabin. The next day they went down to bury Bozeman.

In 1870, friends from Bozeman City reburied him in their town cemetery and held a funeral. His grave made do with a pine board marker until 1883, when pioneer cattleman Nelson Story put up a fine marble marker to his old friend.

Absorkee—
The Second Crow Agency

Located at the Bozeman Trail crossing of the Rosebud Fork of Stillwater River, the agency complex here served as the government's principal point of contact with the Crows from 1875–1882.

It was here that army officers recruited Crow scouts and allies for the campaign against the Sioux in 1876. Such notable frontiersmen as Mitch Boyer, Tom LeForge, and many others headquartered here.

At this time the Yellowstone River served as the boundary of the Crow reservation. Hugo Hoppe built a saloon, trading post, and outfitting point for wolfers and buffalo hunters just across the river north of the agency.

Bernard Thomas painting: *Emigrants on the Bozeman Trail.* Wagons descending toward the Rosebud Fork of the Stillwater River, some three miles south of second Crow Agency.—*Bernard Thomas Collection*

Hunter's Hot Springs

In the early 1870s, Colonel Andrew Jackson Hunter filed on a piece of land around a natural hot spring along the Bozeman Trail's north side route on the Yellowstone. By the time Colonel John Gibbon's men came down the river during the Sioux campaign of 1876, Hunter already had the beginnings of a resort under development. In the early settlement years, it quickly became a popular vacation spot, as well as a place sought for the theraputic effects of its waters. Hunter's spa reached a high level of development when such places were at the peak of popularity in the first quarter of the twentieth century.

Health resort and residence of Dr. A.J. Hunter, Hunter's Hot Springs.—*Montana Historical Society*

Fort Parker—
The First Crow Agency

Crow delegates signed the 1868 Laramie Treaty at several points of contact with the government, many of them at Fort Phil Kearny, others at Fort Laramie, and perhaps a few at Buffalo Rapids on the Yellowstone. The government issued the first annuity goods to the tribe under that agreement in July 1868 near Little Timber Creek. A bit later in the year, Major E.M. Camp, their first resident agent under the treaty, arrived and began construction of an agency on Mission Creek, about twelve miles east of present Livingston.

Due to the high level of hostile Indian activity in the region, Camp had the main agency complex built in the form of a stockaded and bastioned post, similar to the old fur trade forts of some years earlier. He installed a small cannon in one of the bastions.

The agency was the focal point of relations with the Crows, but it served an almost equally important role as a forward base for prospectors, buffalo hunters, wolfers, and for early settlers outside the reservation, along the north bank of the Yellowstone. Charlie Hoffman's trader's store at the agency became important as an outfitter of such expeditions.

By 1873 the Sioux war parties had become bold enough to run off grazing stock within view of the agency.

To get the agency farther from the influence of the teeming civilian traffic in the area, and perhaps to hasten the day when military action against the Sioux would be necessary, the Indian bureau, in early 1875 moved the agency to a point where the Bozeman Trail crossed the Rosebud Fork of Stillwater River.

"Major" Fellows D. Pease served a time as agent to the Crows at "Fort Parker" the first Crow Agency. He stayed on in the country as a trader, and as a partner in trading ventures on the upper Bozeman Trail and down the Yellowstone.
—*Montana Historical Society*

Lieutenant James H. Bradley commanded a detachment of Crow Indian scouts recruited at the Absorkee Agency in 1876. He also wrote some of the best early history of events on the west end of the Bozeman trail.—*Montana Historical Society*

Benson's Landing
On The Yellowstone

There was always heavy traffic on the trails south of the Yellowstone, despite the fact that the commonly accepted route for the Bozeman Trail lies north of the river as far east as the Big Timber area. In 1864, the first Montana Territorial Legislature chartered a company with limitless ambitions, authorizing it to build a wagon road on each of the main trails out of the territory, including the Bozeman and Bridger trails. The company was also authorized to build telegraph lines along these trails to the Pacific Northwest (and on to Alaska to connect with Russian telegraph systems via a Bering Strait cable!), and to build ferryboat operations on the Yellowstone, Clark's Fork, and on the Big Horn. The ferryboat operation was launched in the spring of 1865.

W.J. Davies built the boats on a contract, and received a contract to operate the Yellowstone ferry. He located this first ferry not far below the mouth of the Lower Canyon, about at the upper end of the present town of Livingston, and ran it for several years.

Then in 1868, with a federal subsidy, Billy Lee built a ferry across the Yellowstone a bit further east. Buckskin Frank Williams put up a building nearby, and opened a saloon and trading post. The place quickly became the main point of departure for rough–board "mackinaw" boats departing down the Yellowstone for the States.

Lack of paying customers and harassment by hostile Indians made the ferrymen at Clark's Fork and the Big Horn give up early that season and cache their boats. The Yellowstone ferries, however, continued to do a brisk business.

The community around Billy Lee's ferry had no formal name until Amos Benson and Dan Naileigh built another saloon there in 1875, and from that point onward the place was known as Benson's Landing. Hugo Hoppe built a hotel and saloon at the landing. Skookum Joe Anderson had a trading camp there, and for a time it was the major Montana community, other than Fort Benton, east of the mountains; a real outpost on the frontier.

With the coming of the railroad in 1882–1883, the Northwestern Development Company, an affiliate of the railroad, laid out the townsite of Livingston upstream from the landing, and Benson's with its colorful parade of frontiersmen, and its almost constant harassment by Indians, passed into history.

The Emigrant Gulch Mines

Late in the summer of 1864, prospectors found gold in Emigrant Gulch, not far above the Bozeman Trail on the east side of the Upper Yellowstone Valley. It was difficult ground and production was poor, but many hung on depsite the fact that intinerant traders sold both flour and bacon at a dollar a pound. Never a big producer, the Emigrant Gulch placers continued to attract attention for a long time. As late as 1883, forty men were working these claims with an annual production of aroud twenty-five thousand dollars (equal today to $500,000).

Emigrant Gulch Mining and Chico City, Montana October 1885.—*F. Jay Haynes Photo, Haynes Foundation Collection, Montana Historical Society*

Chico Hot Springs about 1915.—*Museum of the Rockies*

Fort Ellis

On a plain at the foot of Bozeman Pass, the Montana Militia built a stockaded post, Fort Elizabeth Meagher, in 1867. The army took it over when the militia disbanded, renamed it, and rebuilt and expanded the post. It served as the principal defense for Bozeman Pass and that end of the trail, and the main supply point for Fort C.F. Smith.

Thomas Francis Meagher, territorial governor of Montana. The circumstances surrounding his death remain a mystery.—*Montana Historical Society*

Fort Ellis, Montana Territory, July 1875. Drawn by Charles Moellman.—*American Heritage Center, University of Wyoming*

PART SIX

Storm clouds gather over the Big Horn Mountains.—*Jerry Keenan Photo*

The Bozeman Trail Today

To someone flying at moderate elevation in a light aircraft, much of the whole length of the Bozeman Trail would be visible on the ground in the form of ruts left by the endless trains of heavy military supply wagons that often traveled in the spring when the ground was still soft. More than half of the trail mileage remains undisturbed by more recent development!

In places, modern roads follow segments of the trail. Due to the differences in grade requirements, short stretches of the trail are often in view for miles along these modern roads. Most of the sites of military posts and battles along the trail are physically accessible from modern roads, but often they lie on private lands, or on leased state lands, requiring permission for access. Bureau of Land Management offices in Casper, Buffalo, and Billings sell land–status maps that make it possible to determine whether lands are under federal, state or private ownership. U.S. Geological Survey maps are available from those same offices, as well as from many bookstores and engineering supply firms along the way.

Richard's Bridge, the earliest starting point for the Bozeman Trail is easily accessible within the northern edge of the town of Evansville, Wyoming, some five miles east of Casper. Don't miss the special exhibits in the lobby of the U.S. postoffice in Evansville!

The Fort Caspar Museum at the northwest edge of Casper offers exhibits and publications on the history of this immediate area, along with reconstructed 1860s buildings, typical of trading posts in the region during that period.

Bridger's Ferry, perhaps the most important jumping off place for the Bozeman Trail from 1865–1867, lay just downstream from a high bluff on the banks of the North Platte River, about a mile upstream from the interstate highway crossing of that stream near Orin Junction, Wyoming. The relationship of the bluff and the river is about the same today, but many years of occasional flooding, and some farming activity have left no trace of the site.

Fort Fetterman, principal crossing point from the Oregon/California Trail to the Bozeman Trail from September 1867 onward is the best preserved of these Platte Valley sites. Seven miles northeast of Douglas, Wyoming just off state highway 94, the site sits on a level bench overlooking the North Platte River crossing onto the Bozeman Trail.

Two of Fort Fetterman's buildings remain, one of which is a log officer quarters. This may have been a reassembly of logs from buildings built originally at Fort Caspar in 1865. The other building is a unique rammed–earth structure used as an ordnance storehouse. The officer quarters houses a visitor center and museum, while the ordnance storehouse is used for special displays of period vehicles and other large objects.

North from Fort Fetterman the Ross Road is a good graded and graveled road. For most of its length, it closely parallels the Bozeman Trail as far as Antelope Creek. Trail ruts are visible from the road at many points.

At Brown's Springs the road passes within feet of foundation ruins of the 1879 stage station.

The trail from highway 381 down Dry Fork of powder runs at many points right in the stream bed. It would be a very rough trip, even in a good four-wheeled drive vehicle! There is surface evidence of the road ranche at House Creek.

Only scattered bits of trash mark the site of Powder River Crossing on the north side of Dry Fork just east of Powder River. It is on state school land, and lessee permission would be required to visit this site. The river here is fordable *only* in the driest season of the driest years, and then with high clearance vehicles!

On the steady climb up from the Platte River, travelers hardly realized that each new divide was a bit higher than the last until they stood on the last ridge between the South Fork of Cheyenne River and the head of Dry Fork of Powder River. From this point, the windswept prairie rolled off in all directions. The travelers stood amid rocky ridges, dotted with a thin stand of drought stunted pines. A blue line on the eastern horizon marked the Black Hills. Off to the south loomed the Laramie Range that had overlooked their march up the Platte.

Far to the west shimmered the crest of the rugged Big Horns. Close at hand to the north lay the curious, flat-topped Pumpkin Buttes, their crests the durable remnant of what was once the general level of the plains here in distant prehistoric times.

Now the wagons would creak downslope, the sometimes stony, often sandy, bed of the dry wash itself providing the only easy gateway for wagons to the Powder River country. Such terrain made even downhill travel difficult.

Early travelers found this a bleak, thirsty stretch. Colonel Carrington's favorite horse died of poor forage and bad water somewhere along this route in 1866. Travelers from 1876 onward found at least a break in the journey. In early spring 1877, thirty-year army veteran Sergeant Mike Henry took his retirement (Mike had enlisted as a drummer boy in his early teens

Bernard Thomas painting. *Emigrants on the Bozeman Trail.—Bernard Thomas Collection*

for the Mexican War). He put a rough cabin of cottonwood logs at a creek six miles from Powder River. Here, just outside the Cantonment Reno Military Reservation, Henry entertained soldiers and travelers in rough frontier style. To this day, the location is known as "House Creek."

In 1879 the stage line set up a station seventeen

miles from the river and unimaginatively named it Seventeen Mile Station.

The whole area where the Bozeman Trail intersects the main course of Powder River is a main crossroads of frontier activity.

Upstream just a few miles lay the site where Antonio Montero ran a fur trade fort, called "Portu-

guese Houses" from 1834 to 1842, as an agent for the mysterious trader and army intelligence operative Captain Benjamin L.E. Bonneville.

The site of Cantonment Reno/Fort McKinney No. 1 is on federal land administered by the Bureau of Land Management. The outline of the parade ground is marked by depressions on the former sites of dugout buildings, and by a line of smaller depressions further back that mark the lines of outhouses. Collection of artifacts on sites like this is strictly forbidden by federal law. The Bureau of Land Management's Buffalo, Wyoming office administers the site.

Three miles to the north on the graveled road lies the site of Fort Reno. The state of Wyoming owns this

The Bozeman Trail today. The location is between Buffalo and Kaycee. Other than the fence line and road, nothing has changed in the more than one hundred years since covered wagons headed north along the historic Bozeman. In the distance can be seen the snow-capped Big Horn Mountains.—*Jerry Keenan Photo*

Founded in 1878, the John R. Smith ranch was the first filing by a settler in the Powder River country. From a sketch by Merritt D. Houghton.—*Margaret B. Hanson Collection*

site, and it is administered by the Wyoming Recreation Commission. A mound of earth marks the spot where the adobe post commander's quarters weathered away. The site is littered with artifacts, but again, the state antiquities law forbids collecting on this site.

From Fort Reno, a good gravel road closely parallels the Bozeman Trail all the way to Buffalo, Wyoming. The last fifteen or so miles of this road are hard surfaced, and the final few miles follow highway 87.

At Crazy Woman Crossing there is a memorial monument on the creek bank about one-quarter mile downstream from the present bridge. Standing at the monument, one should look to the south, where a high point of hill is skylined. This is the place where Captain George Templeton corralled the wagons of his train for the fight on July 21, 1866. This site is also on BLM land.

At the crossing itself, both up and downstream from the new bridge, emigrant, freighter, and soldier camps were strung out for nearly a mile along the stream.

The site of the Townsend Wagon Train Battle on Soldier Creek is still marked by a cottonwood grove. Some of the trees now there may have been saplings at the time of the fight. The graves of the three men killed here have never been located.

There is a historical marker at the site of August Trabing's 1879–1882 trading post on the west side of the road, a short distance north of the crossing, and an 1890s ranch headquarters several hundred yards away.

Another historical marker stands at the point where the Bozeman Trail crosses Clear Fork near the

Mexican Steer Restaurant at the east edge of Buffalo, just a few hundred yards west of I-90.

Buffalo itself is worth some time. The town is full of 1880s and 1890s structures, most well kept and still in use. The Jim Gatchell Museum houses a massive collection of artifacts from the prehistoric, Bozeman trail, and ranching periods, along with interesting dioramas and interpretive exhibits. Just across the street is the Johnson County Library Annex, housing the western history collections of the library.

Three miles to the west of Buffalo, on Fort Road lies the site of Fort McKinney No. 2. Today, the site is occupied largely by the modern buildings of the Wyoming Soldiers and Sailors Home. Two original structures remain on the site. These are the 1881 Post Hospital and an 1878 infantry barracks.

Running north from Buffalo, I-90 closely parallels the trail for some fifteen miles, and trail ruts are visible at many points. The site of the Nelson Story cattle drive fight at the Rock Creek Crossing is easy to identify because of the ravine-cut bluff to the right of the road.

Lake DeSmet (today much enlarged by dams for irrigation water) lies about two miles east of the highway, and is visible from it. It is a popular boating and fishing site, with excellent catches of trout, yellow perch and a variety of sunfish and rock bass each season.

Interstate 90 crosses the divide into the valley of Piney Creek at exactly the same place as the Bozeman Trail. Take the exit here, and follow old highway 87 north about a mile, watching carefully for signs. A graveled road leads to the west and southwest for about

The post hospital at Fort McKinney built about 1881.— *Author's Photo*

half a mile to the site of Fort Phil Kearny.

This site is owned by the state of Wyoming, and administered by the Wyoming State Museum system. Excellent outdoor exhibits detail the structural layout of the fort and point out the various landmarks that figured in its history. Temporary exhibits are located in a log structure near the site, and a new visitor center is at this writing under development there.

State Highway 1003 leads from the Fort Phil Kearny junction to the picturesque summer home community of Story located in an area of pine timber along Piney Creek, at an elevation of around fifty–five hundred feet. Signs in Story point the way to the Wagon Box Fight site about two miles south of town. There are several memorial markers at the site, marking opposite ends of the wagon corral.

Either I–90 or highway 87 will take one to Sheridan, Wyoming. Highway 87 is the more historic, however, passing the site of the Fetterman fight and the grave of early pioneer E.J. Terril. Three miles south of Sheridan, state highway 331 leads southwest to the village of Big Horn, at the stage road crossing. Today the old stage station/blacksmith shop is a community museum. Big Horn Mercantile has occupied its present building since 1881, one of the oldest continuous businesses in northern Wyoming.

Three miles above Big Horn on Little Goose Creek is the Bradford Brinton Memorial, Quarter–Circle A

Looking north along Highway 87 from the site of the Fetterman fight. Part of the rock fence surrounding the marker may be seen at the extreme right.—*Custer Battlefield National Monument*

Big Horn, Wyoming.—*Elsa Spear Bryon Photo*

Ranch. Started as a horse ranch by the Moncrieffe family in the 1890s, it was the home of industrialist Bradford Brinton from 1920–1936. The house and an adjacent gallery house one of the major collections of western art in the region, and it is open daily during the summer months.

At the middle interchange of I–90 in Sheridan is the Wyoming Highway Commission and Sheridan Chamber of Commerce visitor center. Here a relief model of the Big Horn Mountains and the foothill country along with historical and other exhibits, enables one to get a quick view of the scenic and recreation resources of the region.

Seventeen miles northwest of Sheridan is the Ranchester interchange. For the last few miles after crossing the Tongue River Bridge, the interstate moves virtually in the tracks of the Bozeman Trail.

At Ranchester, watch for signs. Conner Battlefield State Historical Park lies just across Tongue River via a county highway bridge. In this cottonwood grove, Connor's men had their epic fight with the Arapahos on August 29, 1865. A memorial marker and interpretive sign describes the event.

From Ranchester, one can also take U.S. Highway 14, west six miles along the Bozeman Trail to Dayton. At about the half-way point is the site and interpretive sign for the Sawyers Wagon Train Fight of 1865. Francois LaRocque in 1805 and Charles LeRaye in 1802 both crossed Tongue River at this point, and LaRocque camped here for several days, while his Crow Indian companions hunted bears.

Just east of the Tongue River Bridge a county road turns north, paralleling the Bozeman Trail for part of its way back to U.S. Highway 87. Highway 87 parallels the Bozeman trail to the vicinity of the Montana boundary.

To reach the "horseback" or trapper route of the Bozeman Trail, traversed first by wagons in the 1859 Raynolds Expedition, one must turn off at the last gravel road to the west within Wyoming, and travel about ten miles to a point where the trail picks up the alignment of the present road. The road goes right in the former trail ruts (a good graveled road) down to the Little Horn at the mouth of the Red Canyon. Raynolds' description of this route makes it instantly recognizable. However, it is not practicable to follow the route beyond this point, for private and Indian lands predominate, complex permissions would be required, and the terrain has always been difficult for vehicles.

Another segment of the Bozeman Trail may be seen by going up the Lodge Grass Creek Road some miles to a point where, on the right, deep wagon ruts stand out in a very steep trail over a high "hogback" ridge. Back on the Little Horn, a modern hard-surface road reaches the Little Horn crossing of the Bozeman Trail.

Trail crossings at Rotten Grass Creek and at Soap

Creek, as mapped are accessible by fair country roads.

The early heavy wagon route of the Bozeman Trail follows down a ridge between Prairie Dog Creek and Goose Creek, just east of I-90.

It crosses Tongue River and follows the north side of the stream to a point near Dayton, Wyoming, where it joins a shortcut for wagons coming across country from Big Horn, Wyoming, as well as the early horseback route that follows small stream drainages close to the foot of the mountains.

From this point, the horseback route sticks closer to the mountain, whereas the wagon route runs well out in the rough foothill country, generally staying high on ridges that provided steep but firm hills and well drained trail, with a minimum number of stream crossings.

The two trails cross the Big Horn together at Fort C.F. Smith, with one alternative crossing used by early wagons near the mouth of Soap Creek.

At this writing, the site of Fort C.F. Smith is under archeological investigation for historic site development by the National Park Service. The sites of the Wagon Box Fight and Fort Phil Kearny are owned by the state of Wyoming. All three locations are well marked.

Beyond the Big Horn, the Bozeman Trail runs between Beauvais Coulee and the mountain, paralleled closely by a good graveled road. The trail crosses Pryor Creek and the Pryor Road at that village. Just upstream about three miles is the restored home of Chief Plenty Coups, a famous Crow Indian, and nearby is an interesting museum devoted to Crow history.

From Pryor, the trail runs almost straight west to Edgar, Montana, and then well away from modern roads, it heads northwest, with one branch crossing the Yellowstone near Big Timber, and another following not far south of the river. Both branches join at Benson's Landing just east of Livingston, Montana.

From that point the trail heads up over Bozeman Pass. Three miles east of Bozeman is an historical marker at the site of Fort Ellis.

In Bozeman, a small museum at the courthouse displays many Bozeman Trail items, running clear back to fur trade days. In front of the building is the Big Horn Gun, a 6-pounder howitzer used by prospectors in the 1870s.

At Montana State University in Bozeman, the Museum of the Rockies is a major regional museum of natural history, archeology, and history of the region.

An extension of the trail runs near present roads to Virginia City, a restored mining town. Not many incidents happened along this route, as it lay in the range of the friendly Crows in a country that was settling up fast in the 1860s.

Virginia City, Montana Territory. The end of the trail, from a pencil sketch by A.E. Mathews.— *Montana Historical Society*

Suggested Reading List

Annini, James. *They Gazed on the Beartooths*, privately printed, n.d.

Bourke, John G. *Mackenzie's Last Fight with the Cheyennes*, Fort Collins: Old Army Press, 1968.

Bratt, John. *Trails of Yesterday*, Chicago: University Publ., 1921. The story of a freighter and log contractor employee who wintered at the post in 1866-1867.

Brown, Dee. *Fort Phil Kearny*, N.Y.: Putnam, 1962.

———. *The Fetterman Massacre*, Lincoln: University of Nebraska, 1973.

Carrington, Frances Courtney Grummond. *My Army Life*, New York: Lippincott, 1911.

Carrington, Margaret. *Absaraka, Home of the Crows*, Chicago: Lakeside Press, 1950.

Heberd, Grace R., and E.A. Brininstool. *The Bozeman Trail*, Glendale: Arthur H. Clark Co., 1922.

Mattes, Merrill J. *Indians, Infants and Infantry*, Denver: Old West, 1963. The story of an army family who lived at Fort C.F. Smith.

Murray, Robert A. *Military Posts in the Powder River of Wyoming 1865–1894*, Lincoln: University of Nebraska Press, 1968.

———. *Army on Powder River*, Fort Collins: Old Army Press, 1970.

———. *Johnson County, Wyoming, 175 Years of History at the Foot of the Big Horn Mountains*, Buffalo, Wy.: Chamber of Commerce, 1981.

Ostrander, A.B. *An Army Boy of the Sixties*, Yonkers: N.Y., World Book Company, 1926.

———. *The Bozeman Trail Forts under General Philip St. George Cooke*, Seattle. Privately printed, 1932.

Smith, Helena Huntington, *War on Powder River*, N.Y.: McGraw-Hill, 1966. The story of the early settlement era and the Johnson County invasion.

Straight, Michael. *Carrington*. New York: 1962. Fiction, but very skillful, historical, and carefully researched. Several editions.

Vaughn, J.W. *With Crook at the Rosebud*, Harrisburg, Pa. Stackpole, 1956.

———. *Indian Fights, New Facts on Seven Encounters*, Norman: University of Oklahoma Press, 1967.

Topping, E.S. Robert A. Murray, ed. *Chronicles of the Yellowstone*, Mpls.: Ross & Raines, 1968.

Index